FREE

Free Study Tips DVD

In addition to the tips and content in this guide, we have created a FREE DVD with helpful study tips to further assist your exam preparation. **This FREE Study Tips DVD provides you with top-notch tips to conquer your exam and reach your goals.**

Our simple request in exchange for the strategy-packed DVD is that you email us your feedback about our study guide. We would love to hear what you thought about the guide, and we welcome any and all feedback—positive, negative, or neutral. It is our #1 goal to provide you with top quality products and customer service.

To receive your **FREE Study Tips DVD**, email freedvd@apexprep.com. Please put "FREE DVD" in the subject line and put the following in the email:

a. The name of the study guide you purchased.

b. Your rating of the study guide on a scale of 1-5, with 5 being the highest score.

c. Any thoughts or feedback about your study guide.

d. Your first and last name and your mailing address, so we know where to send your free DVD!

Thank you!

LSAT Prep Books 2021-2022

The LSAT Tutor Exam Study Guide and Official Practice Test [4th Edition]

Matthew Lanni

Written and edited by APEX Publishing.

ISBN 13: 9781628459449
ISBN 10: 1628459441

APEX Publishing is not connected with or endorsed by any official testing organization. APEX Publishing creates and publishes unofficial educational products. All test and organization names are trademarks of their respective owners.

The material in this publication is included for utilitarian purposes only and does not constitute an endorsement by APEX Publishing of any particular point of view.

For additional information or for bulk orders, contact info@apexprep.com.

Table of Contents

Test Taking Strategies

1. Reading the Whole Question

A popular assumption in Western culture is the idea that we don't have enough time for anything. We speed while driving to work, we want to read an assignment for class as quickly as possible, or we want the line in the supermarket to dwindle faster. However, speeding through such events robs us from being able to thoroughly appreciate and understand what's happening around us. While taking a timed test, the feeling one might have while reading a question is to find the correct answer as quickly as possible. Although pace is important, don't let it deter you from reading the whole question. Test writers know how to subtly change a test question toward the end in various ways, such as adding a negative or changing focus. If the question has a passage, carefully read the whole passage as well before moving on to the questions. This will help you process the information in the passage rather than worrying about the questions you've just read and where to find them. A thorough understanding of the passage or question is an important way for test takers to be able to succeed on an exam.

2. Examining Every Answer Choice

Let's say we're at the market buying apples. The first apple we see on top of the heap may *look* like the best apple, but if we turn it over we can see bruising on the skin. We must examine several apples before deciding which apple is the best. Finding the correct answer choice is like finding the best apple. Some exams ask for the *best* answer choice, which means that there are several choices that could be correct, but one choice is always better than the rest. Although it's tempting to choose an answer that seems correct at first without reading the others, it's important to read each answer choice thoroughly before making a final decision on the answer. The aim of a test writer might be to get as close as possible to the correct answer, so watch out for subtle words that may indicate an answer is incorrect. Once the correct answer choice is selected, read the question again and the answer in response to make sure all your bases are covered.

3. Eliminating Wrong Answer Choices

Sometimes we become paralyzed when we are confronted with too many choices. Which frozen yogurt flavor is the tastiest? Which pair of shoes look the best with this outfit? What type of car will fill my needs as a consumer? If you are unsure of which answer would be the best to choose, it may help to use process of elimination. We use "filtering" all the time on sites such as eBay® or Craigslist® to eliminate the ads that are not right for us. We can do the same thing on an exam. Process of elimination is crossing out the answer choices we know for sure are wrong and leaving the ones that might be correct. It may help to cover up the incorrect answer choices with a piece of paper, although if the exam is computer-based, you may have to use your hand or mentally cross out the incorrect answer choices. Covering incorrect choices is a psychological act that alleviates stress due to the brain being exposed to a smaller amount of information. Choosing between two answer choices is much easier than choosing between four or five, and you have a better chance of selecting the correct answer if you have less to focus on.

4. Sticking to the World of the Question

When we are attempting to answer questions, our minds will often wander away from the question and what it is asking. We begin to see answer choices that are true in the real world instead of true in the world of the question. It may be helpful to think of each test question as its own little world. This world may be different from ours. This world may know as a truth that the chicken came before the egg or may assert that two plus two equals five. Remember that, no matter what hypothetical nonsense may be in the question, assume it to be true. If the question states that the chicken came before the egg, then choose your answer based on that truth. Sticking to the world of the question means placing all of our biases and assumptions aside and relying on the question to guide us to the correct answer. If we are simply looking for answers that are correct based on our own judgment, then we may choose incorrectly. Remember an answer that is true does not necessarily answer the question.

5. Key Words

If you come across a complex test question that you have to read over and over again, try pulling out some key words from the question in order to understand what exactly it is asking. Key words may be words that surround the question, such as *main idea, analogous, parallel, resembles, structured,* or *defines.* The question may be asking for the main idea, or it may be asking you to define something. Deconstructing the sentence may also be helpful in making the question simpler before trying to answer it. This means taking the sentence apart and obtaining meaning in pieces, or separating the question from the foundation of the question. For example, let's look at this question:

Given the author's description of the content of paleontology in the first paragraph, which of the following is most parallel to what it taught?

The question asks which one of the answers most *parallels* the following information: The *description* of paleontology in the first paragraph. The first step would be to see *how* paleontology is described in the first paragraph. Then, we would find an answer choice that parallels that description. The question seems complex at first, but after we deconstruct it, the answer becomes much more attainable.

6. Subtle Negatives

Negative words in question stems will be words such as *not, but, neither,* or *except.* Test writers often use these words in order to trick unsuspecting test takers into selecting the wrong answer—or, at least, to test their reading comprehension of the question. Many exams will feature the negative words in all caps (*which of the following is NOT an example*), but some questions will add the negative word seamlessly into the sentence. The following is an example of a subtle negative used in a question stem:

According to the passage, which of the following is *not* considered to be an example of paleontology?

If we rush through the exam, we might skip that tiny word, *not,* inside the question, and choose an answer that is opposite of the correct choice. Again, it's important to read the question fully, and double check for any words that may negate the statement in any way.

7. Spotting the Hedges

The word "hedging" refers to language that remains vague or avoids absolute terminology. Absolute terminology consists of words like *always, never, all, every, just, only, none,* and *must.* Hedging refers to words like *seem, tend, might, most, some, sometimes, perhaps, possibly, probability,* and *often.* In some cases, we want to choose answer choices that use hedging and avoid answer choices that use absolute terminology. Of course, this always depends on what subject you are being tested on. Humanities subjects like history and literature will contain hedging, because those subjects often do not have absolute answers. However, science and math may contain absolutes that are necessary for the question to be answered. It's important to pay attention to what subject you are on and adjust your response accordingly.

8. Restating to Understand

Every now and then we come across questions that we don't understand. The language may be too complex, or the question is structured in a way that is meant to confuse the test taker. When you come across a question like this, it may be worth your time to rewrite or restate the question in your own words in order to understand it better. For example, let's look at the following complicated question:

Which of the following words, if substituted for the word *parochial* in the first paragraph, would LEAST change the meaning of the sentence?

Let's restate the question in order to understand it better. We know that they want the word *parochial* replaced. We also know that this new word would "least" or "not" change the meaning of the sentence. Now let's try the sentence again:

Which word could we replace with *parochial,* and it would not change the meaning?

Restating it this way, we see that the question is asking for a synonym. Now, let's restate the question so we can answer it better:

Which word is a synonym for the word *parochial*?

Before we even look at the answer choices, we have a simpler, restated version of a complicated question. Remember that, if you have paper, you can always rewrite the simpler version of the question so as not to forget it.

9. Guessing

When is it okay to guess on an exam? This question depends on the test format of the particular exam you're taking. On some tests, answer choices that are answered incorrectly are penalized. If you know that you are penalized for wrong answer choices, avoid guessing on the test question. If you can narrow the question down to fifty percent by process of elimination, then perhaps it may be worth it to guess between two answer choices. But if you are unsure of the correct answer choice among three or four answers, it may help to leave the question unanswered. Likewise, if the exam you are taking does *not* penalize for wrong answer choices, answer the questions first you know to be true, then go back through and mark an answer choice, even if you do not know the correct answer. This way, you will at least have a one in four chance of getting the answer correct. It may also be helpful to do some research on the exam you plan to take in order to understand how the questions are graded.

10. Avoiding Patterns

One popular myth in grade school relating to standardized testing is that test writers will often put multiple-choice answers in patterns. A runoff example of this kind of thinking is that the most common answer choice is "C," with "B" following close behind. Or, some will advocate certain made-up word patterns that simply do not exist. Test writers do not arrange their correct answer choices in any kind of pattern; their choices are randomized. There may even be times where the correct answer choice will be the same letter for two or three questions in a row, but we have no way of knowing when or if this might happen. Instead of trying to figure out what choice the test writer probably set as being correct, focus on what the *best answer choice* would be out of the answers you are presented with. Use the tips above, general knowledge, and reading comprehension skills in order to best answer the question, rather than looking for patterns that do not exist.

FREE DVD OFFER

Achieving a high score on your exam depends not only on understanding the content, but also on understanding how to apply your knowledge and your command of test taking strategies. **Because your success is our primary goal, we offer a FREE Study Tips DVD, which provides top-notch test taking strategies to help you optimize your testing experience.**

Our simple request in exchange for the strategy-packed DVD is that you email us your feedback about our study guide.

To receive your **FREE Study Tips DVD**, email freedvd@apexprep.com. Please put "FREE DVD" in the subject line and put the following in the email:

a. The name of the study guide you purchased.

b. Your rating of the study guide on a scale of 1-5, with 5 being the highest score.

c. Any thoughts or feedback about your study guide.

d. Your first and last name and your mailing address, so we know where to send your free DVD!

Introduction to the LSAT

Function of the Test

The Law School Admission Test (LSAT) is a required component of the application process to nearly all law schools in the United States that are accredited by the American Board Association (ABA). There may be other unaccredited law schools and a few accredited ones that accept GRE scores instead of LSAT scores, but for all intents and purposes, LSAT scores are necessary for consideration of admission to all Juris Doctor (JD) programs in the country. Accordingly, nearly all test takers are prospective candidates for JD programs in in the United States, Canada, and certain other countries.

The test is designed and administered by the Law School Admission Council (LSAC). Like the SAT, GRE, and other standardized tests used primarily for the admissions process to educational institutions, the LSAT does not have a set "passing score." Instead, minimum scores and the importance of the score (its weight) in deciding a candidate's acceptance into the program is determined by each individual law program. Scores are typically considered alongside other criteria such as courses taken, GPA, personal recommendations, among other things.

The LSAC reports that score distributions, which follow a normal bell curve, remain very stable from year to year.

Test Administration

The Digital LSAT will be offered nine times in the 2019-2020 testing year. There are hundreds of available testing locations around the United States, Canada, and many other countries; however, the dates may vary.

It is recommended that candidates register for the exam on or before the posted deadlines in order to optimize the chances of receiving their preferred date and location. The base fee for taking the test is $200, with additional fees for students requesting late registration, a test center change, hand scoring of their exam, or other services. If a student wishes to take a standalone LSAT writing test, the cost is $15.

The LSAC offers a variety of accommodations for test takers with documented disabilities. It is important to note that a candidate seeking accommodations must register for the LSAT first before submitting documentation in support of his or her disabilities. Registration must be completed prior to the deadline in order to request accommodations. The necessary forms and materials are available on the LSAC website (https://www.lsac.org/jd/lsat/accommodated-testing).

The Law School Admission Council (LSAC) permits students to take the LSAT no more than three times in a single testing year and no more than five times in a five-year time period including the current and five past testing years. The LSAT can be taken a total of seven times in a student's lifetime. This is a new policy as of September 2019; therefore, tests taken previously to September 2019 will not count against these limits. LSAC does evaluate requests for exceptions based on extenuating circumstances on a case-by-case basis.

Test Format

There are five thirty-five-minute sections comprised of multiple-choice questions on the LSAT. Four of the sections—a Reading Comprehension section, an Analytical Reasoning section, and two Logical Reasoning sections—are scored, and one section—the "variable" section—is unscored. This variable section contains material that the test developers are testing out for consideration on future exams. While taking the exam, test takers are not informed about which section contains the unscored, pretest questions, though this information is divulged on the score report.

The LSAT is now offered in digital format and is taken on electronic tablets provided by the testing center. Students choose their answers by tapping on their selected answer choice on the screen. The new format allows for highlighting and flagging through the use of a touchscreen. Scratch paper and a pen will be provided for test takers to make notes during the test. Test takers may also use their own pencil and eraser during the test. The Digital LSAT has multiple-choice exam sections with similar structure and content to the traditional pen and paper exam.

The LSAT Writing test is not completed on the same day as the other sections but is completed on the test taker's own electronic device online using a secure testing platform at a time and place convenient to the test taker. The LSAT writing still uses a decision-prompt structure similar to that from the previous LSAT writing exams. Test takers are still given thirty-five minutes to complete their sample. The writing test is not scored, but copies of the sample produced are provided to all schools to which the student applies.

Scoring

A candidate's raw score on the LSAT is calculated by totaling the number of questions that he or she answered correctly. All sections and questions are weighted equally. Incorrect responses are not penalized, so the test taker incurs no risk by guessing. A test taker's raw score is then scaled to the standard LSAT score from 120 to 180. This scaling process accounts for differences in difficulty between test forms and allows scores to be compared.

Although there is no set passing score, obtaining high scores is important for candidates seeking admission to competitive law programs. The typical LSAT score for a student accepted to a moderately competitive law school hovers around 145 or 150, while the most competitive law schools are usually looking for LSAT scores of 165 or higher. Although candidates can retake the test a couple of times, schools receive all grades and often take the average score into consideration rather than the highest score. There is also a risk of receiving a lower score on a retest, and since schools will also receive this score, candidates should be judicious in their decisions to retake the LSAT.

Important

The practice test begins on page 71. This practice test is officially licensed from the Law School Admission Council (LSAC) and appeared in a previous LSAT exam. You can take the practice test with confidence, knowing that it was created by LSAC.

Throughout the study guide content, prior to page 71, there are sample questions created by APEX Test Prep. These questions are not official practice questions and were NOT created by LSAC. The only official LSAC questions are in the practice test that begins on page 71.

All actual LSAT® content reproduced within this work is used with the permission of Law School Admission Council, Inc., (LSAC) Box 40, Newtown, PA 18940, the copyright owner. LSAC does not review or endorse specific test-preparation materials, companies, or services, and inclusion of licensed LSAT content within this work does not imply the review or endorsement of LSAC. LSAT is a registered trademark of LSAC.

LSAT Logical Reasoning

The LSAT contains two Logical Reasoning sections, both with 25 questions, so this section comprises a significant portion of the test. The questions in the Logical Reasoning section of the LSAT evaluate the test taker's ability to critically consider, analyze, and complete various arguments presented in common language. These skills are paramount to the success of a law student and future attorney, who must develop a strong foundation of critical reasoning skills. Lawyers are constantly tasked with evaluating, analyzing, building, and refuting arguments and identifying gaps, inconsistencies, fallacies, and assumptions in such arguments.

The LSAT test developers design the arguments and their associated questions in the Logical Reasoning section to require the same type of legal reasoning that prospective law students will encounter in their studies and careers. Rather than using legalese and law as a subject matter, for the most part, questions are based on short arguments that address ordinary situations in common language, such as those found in newspapers, academic publications, advertisements, media of various kinds, and magazines.

It is useful for test takers to bear in mind that the questions on the LSAT do not require specialized outside knowledge. For example, even if the argument addresses the viability of renewable energy sources, the test taker does not need prior background in energy sources to successfully answer the question. The LSAT is designed to specifically assess how one considers and analyzes premises, not their familiarity with particular subject matter. In fact, it is important for test takers to avoid viewing the concepts in the argument in the context of their own prior knowledge, opinions, or beliefs. Instead, they should only consider the closed system of the presented argument and associated question.

The exercises in the Logical Reasoning not only contain sufficient information to correctly answer the questions, but they also allow test takers to determine which part of the question (the argument or the provided answer choices) should be assumed to be "true" and used as the benchmark against which the other part should be evaluated. The question stem in a Logical Reasoning question can potentially establish one of two different relationships between the argument and the provided answer choices: either the argument is stated as truth and the answer choices are evaluated in accordance to it, or each of the five answer choices are asserted as truths, and the positive or negative effect of each choice on the argument must be evaluated.

Logical Reasoning: Tips for Success

Unlike the other two sections, each Logical Reasoning question stands alone, meaning it's answered independently from the rest of the section. Consequently, test takers have more freedom in how they choose to strategically attack this section. As such, it's advisable to practice under time constraints and conditions that mirror the test day environment. This helps in developing and executing a game plan that balances efficiency with accuracy.

The first thing to consider when crafting a game plan is time. Because the Logical Reasoning section typically includes twenty-five questions to be answered in thirty-five minutes, this leaves an average of a little less than 1.5 minutes per question. As a general rule of thumb, Logical Reasoning questions tend to become progressively more difficult throughout the section. So, it's best to knock out the early questions as efficiently as possible. Many successful test takers try to establish a benchmark for the beginning portion, like completing the first ten questions in ten minutes, which leaves more time for the more difficult questions.

Always read the question first. The questions are almost always brief, or at least significantly shorter than the stimulus argument; therefore, reading the question first gives test takers a preview as to what they should be looking for without sacrificing much time. This reduces the likelihood that you'll need to read the argument multiple times.

Many test takers use annotations or some type of shorthand to better understand the stimulus argument. For example, you might find it worthwhile to underline the conclusions. Aside from comprehension, annotations can also speed up the time it takes to read the argument a second time, which might be necessary after going through the answer choices.

Consider all of the answer choices before finalizing an answer. The test makers usually include several choices that look appealing on the surface, but one answer will stand out from the rest. Along the way, remember to cross out clearly wrong answer choices to increase the probability of guessing correctly if time or difficulty forces your hand.

To help avoid a time crunch, you should figure out when it's most efficient to cut your losses on difficult questions. Here are a couple useful indicators for when you should probably skip ahead and come back later. First, if you don't understand the stimulus at all after your initial read through, then it might be best to skip ahead. Second, if another pass at the argument doesn't bring any clarity, then it's definitely time to move on. Third, if you understand the argument but can't seem to eliminate any answer choices, then your time might be better spent on different questions. Remember all of the questions are worth the same amount of points. One of the biggest mistakes test takers commit is wasting five or more minutes on a single question.

Finally, if you're running out of time, start answering questions with the shortest stimulus argument. Parallel reasoning and parallel flaw type questions should also be left for last when time is running out, even if they appear to be brief. These questions almost always require the most time because they force the test taker to break down and compare the stimulus argument with five additional arguments. One exception to the rule is to answer all of the question types that you know best. For example, if you're amazing at necessary assumption questions, then make sure to do all of them before time runs out. The LSAT tests time management as much as anything else, so come with a plan but adjust accordingly as conditions change on the ground.

Recognizing Parts of an Argument and Their Relationships

Premise and Conclusion
Not all arguments on the LSAT Logical Reasoning section are true "arguments"; some are merely collections of factual statements strung together. For this reason, some texts use the term *stimulus* to describe the text part of a problem that precedes the question and answer choices, as *argument* can be a misnomer.

Stimuli that are true arguments contain a *conclusion* that is derived from statements called *premises*, which give reasons why whatever is asserted in the conclusion should be believed. For example, consider the following simple argument:

All basketball players are tall. Christopher is a basketball player. Therefore, Christopher is tall.

In this short argument, the first two statements provide the reasons to accept the third statement. Thus, the premises are: *All basketball players are tall*, and *Christopher is a basketball player*. The conclusion is: *Christopher is tall.*

It is worth mentioning again that some arguments presented on the LSAT may contain factual inaccuracies or opinions that test takers disagree with. The LSAT test developers purposely design certain exercises in this manner to try and trip up test takers who draw upon their own knowledge, common sense, or experience. It is important to remember that the test is evaluating one's ability to reason logically and use provided "evidence," rather than assess their opinions and subject area expertise.

Assumption

In the structure of an argument, an *assumption* is an unstated premise. Many Logical Reasoning questions will ask you to identify the assumption within arguments, and you must find something that the argument is relying on that the author is not stating explicitly. Many strengthening and weakening questions deal with unstated assumptions, as well as necessary and sufficient assumption questions. Let's take a look at what an unstated assumption looks like:

All restaurants in the Seattle area serve vegan food. *Haile's Seafood* must serve vegan food.

Let's identify all parts of the argument, including the unstated assumption. The conclusion of this argument is the last sentence: *Haile's Seafood* must serve vegan food. The premise we are given is the first sentence: All restaurants in the Seattle area serve vegan food. Now let's ask ourselves if there's a missing link. How did the author reach this conclusion? The author reached this conclusion with an unstated assumption, which might look like this: *Haile's Seafood* is in the Seattle area. Now we have the argument:

Premise: All restaurants in the Seattle area serve vegan food.

Unstated Assumption: *Haile's Seafood* is in the Seattle area.

Conclusion: *Haile's Seafood* must serve vegan food

Another way to look at the missing link is like this: there is a connection between "Seattle area" and "vegan food," and one between *"Haile's Seafood"* and "vegan food", but there is no connection between "Seattle area" and *"Haile's Seafood."* The unstated assumption identifies this connection.

Fact Sets

Stimuli that are fact sets rather than arguments contain a group of statements but lack any sort of conclusion. For example, consider the following fact set:

There are three elementary schools in town. Fort River has 240 students. Wildwood has 275 students. Crocker Farm has 180 students.

An argument, by definition, must include a conclusion; therefore, the prior four sentences do not constitute an argument because no conclusion is presented. Instead, the statements simply assert facts about the elementary schools without inflicting judgement or answering *so what?* One useful tip for test takers to determine whether the stimulus contains an argument or a fact set is to evaluate, on a very basic level, whether they feel a reaction after reading. Fact sets, by nature, do not evoke much of an emotional response and read more like a list of assertions with no obvious "point." Arguments, on the other hand, often draw readers in more, causing them to "care," question, disagree, or otherwise evoke some sort of emotional reaction.

Again, arguments must contain a conclusion, which is a judgement or statement that the author wants readers to believe given one or multiple reasons (premises) that serve as evidence or tools to persuade the readers to accept the conclusion. The conclusion is commonly signaled by words such as *so, therefore,* thus, *for this reason, accordingly, hence, shows that, consequently, as a result,* etc. Words that are commonly indicative of premises include *because, for, since, in order to, for example, as indicated by, owing to, due to, this is evidenced by,* etc. While premises and conclusions are often signaled by these words and phrases, they do not always include such explicit indicators.

When stimuli are true arguments, it is critical to identify the conclusion prior to considering the answer choices to the question because the crux of the question often lies in the conclusion. Failing to fully grasp and mentally consider the conclusion can cause unfocused test takers to fall for red herrings or answer choices purposely designed to contain just small inaccuracies or inconsistencies from the conclusion or premises.

Tricks, Fallacies, and Flaws in Arguments

In some question stems, the LSAT test designers will ask you to identify some type of flaw in an argument's reasoning. The question is not really asking for information to strengthen or weaken the statement, or an assumption to validate the conclusion, like the strengthen, weaken, or assumption questions. Rather, argument flaw questions want you to provide a description of that error. In order for you to be able to describe what flaw is occurring in the argument, it will help to know of various argumentative flaws, such as red herring, false choice, and correlation vs. causation. We will look at those below. Here are some examples of what Flaw Questions look like:

- The reasoning in the argument is flawed because the argument . . .
- The argument is most vulnerable to criticism on the grounds that it . . .
- Which one of the following is an error in the argument's reasoning?
- A flaw in the reasoning of the argument is that . . .
- Which one of the following most accurately describes X's criticism of the argument made by Y?

Bait/Switch
One common flaw that is good to know is called the "bait and switch." It occurs when the test makers will provide an argument that offers evidence about X, and ends the argument with a conclusion about Y. A "bait and switch" answer choice will look like this:

The argument assumes that X does in fact address Y without providing justification.

Let's look at an example:

Hannah will most likely always work out and maintain a healthy physique. After all, Hannah's IQ is extremely high.

The correct answer will look like this:

The argument assumes that Hannah's high IQ addresses her likelihood of always working out without providing justification.

Ascriptive Error
The ascriptive argument will begin the argument with something a third party has claimed. Usually, it will be something very general, like "Some people say that . . ." or "Generally, it has been said . . ." Then, the arguer will follow up that claim with a refutation or opposing view. The problem here is that when the

arguer phrases something in this general sense without a credible source, their refutation of that evidence doesn't really matter. Here's an example:

It has been said that peppermint oil has been proven to relieve stomach issues and, in some cases, prevent cancer. I can attest to the relief in stomach issues; however, there is just not enough evidence to prove whether or not peppermint oil has the ability to prevent any kind of cancerous cells from forming in the body.

The correct answer will look like this:

> The argument assumes that the refuting evidence matters to the position that is being challenged.
>
> We have no credible source in this argument, so the refutation is senseless.

Prescriptive Error

First, let's take a look at what "prescriptive" means. Prescriptive means to give directions, or to say something *ought to* or *should* do something else. On the LSAT, sometimes an argument will be a descriptive premise (simply describing) that leads to a prescriptive conclusion, which makes for a very weak argument. This is like saying "There is a hurricane coming; therefore, we should leave the state." Even though this seems like common sense, the logical soundness of this argument is missing. A valid argument is when the truth of the premise leads absolutely to the truth of the conclusion. It's when the conclusion *is* something, not when the conclusion *should* be or do something. The flaw here is the assumption that the conclusion is going to work out; something prescriptive is not ever guaranteed to work out in a logical argument.

False Choice

A false choice, or false dilemma, flaw on the LSAT is a statement that assumes only the object it lists in the statement is the solution, or the only options that exist, for that problem. Here is an example:

> I didn't get the grade I want in Chemistry class. I must either be really stupid, I didn't get enough sleep, or I didn't eat enough that day.

This is a false choice error. We are offered only three options for why the speaker did not get the grade he or she wanted in Chemistry class. However, there is potentially more options why the grade was not achieved other than the three listed. The speaker could have been fighting a cold, or the professor may not have taught the material in a comprehensive way. It is our job as test takers to recognize that there are more options other than the choices we are given, although it appears that the only three choices are listed in the example.

Red Herring

A red herring is a point offered in an argument that is only meant to distract or mislead. A red herring will throw something out after the argument that is unrelated to the argument, although it still commands attention, thus taking attention away from the relevant issue. The following is an example of a red herring fallacy:

Kirby: It seems like therapy is moving toward a more holistic model rather than something prescriptive, where the space between a therapist and client is seen more organic rather than a controlled space. This helps empower the client to reach their own conclusions about what should be done rather than having someone tell them what to do.

Barlock: What's the point of therapy anyway? It seems like "talking out" problems with a stranger is a waste of time and always has been. Is it even successful as a profession?

We see Kirby present an argument about the route therapy is taking toward the future. Instead of responding to the argument by presenting their own side regarding where therapy is headed, Barlock questions the overall point of therapy. Barlock throws out a red herring here: Kirby cannot proceed with the argument because now Kirby must defend the existence of therapy instead of its future.

Correlation Versus Causality

The LSAT test developers frequently make use of cause-and-effect reasoning in arguments to explain why something has or has not occurred. Test takers should be careful when reviewing causal conclusions because the reasoning is often flawed, incorrectly classifying correlation as causality. In many Logical Reasoning arguments (as well as real-world situations), two events that may or may not be associated with one another are said to be linked such that one was the cause or reason for the other, which is considered the effect. To be a true "cause-and-effect" relationship, one factor or event must occur first (the cause) and be the sole reason (unless others are also listed) that the other occurred (the effect). The cause serves as the initiator of the relationship between the two events.

For example, consider the following argument:

> Last weekend, the local bakery ran out of blueberry muffins and some customers had to select something else instead. This week, the bakery's sales have fallen. Therefore, the blueberry muffin shortage last weekend resulted in fewer sales this week.

In this argument, the author states that the decline in sales this week (the effect) was caused by the shortage of blueberry muffins last weekend. However, there are other viable alternate causes for the decline in sales this week besides the blueberry muffin shortage. Perhaps it is summer and many normal patrons are away this week on vacation, or maybe another local bakery just opened or is running a special sale this week. There might be a large construction project or road work in town near the bakery, deterring customers from navigating the detours or busy roads. It is entirely possible that the decline this week is just a random coincidence and not attributable to any factor other than chance, and that next week, sales will return to normal or even exceed typical sales. Insufficient evidence exists to confidently assert that the blueberry muffin shortage was the sole reason for the decline in sales, thus mistaking correlation for causation.

Extreme Language

Test makers often include *extreme language* in the stimulus arguments, questions, and answer choices. Depending on usage and context, extreme language can function as a useful guide to finding the correct answer, eliminating incorrect answer choices, and avoiding traps that look very appealing upon first glance.

Extreme language generally falls into two different categories. First, absolute extreme language indicates that something is an all or nothing proposition. Examples of common absolutes include: *all, always, certainly, each, every, whenever, none, never,* and *cannot.* Second, descriptors related to likelihood, quality, or quantity are used to heighten language in an extreme way. Words that denote superiority or importance compared to some other thing include: *chief, exceedingly, greatest, hardly, main, most, nearly all, primarily* and *typically.*

In contrast, nonextreme language is softer, such as describing an event as a possibility rather than a probability. Examples of nonextreme language include: *a few*, *approximately*, *around*, *at least*, *at times*, *generally*, *might*, *occasionally*, and *sometimes*. Oftentimes the test makers' decision to use nonextreme language is just as revealing as extreme language. Consider the following sentences:

> LeBron James is the greatest basketball player of all time.

> LeBron James is a great basketball player.

Both sentences tell us that someone named LeBron James is a talented basketball player; however, the first sentence goes much further, indicating that LeBron James is superior to all of his competition. If a stimulus argument includes this sentence and then names another basketball player, we know LeBron James is better at basketball than the other player, whether that's specifically mentioned or not. In effect, the extreme language in the first sentence is creating a conditional. If there is another basketball player, then they must not be as good as LeBron James.

Conditionals are another type of extreme language because they are outcome determinative. Whenever the conditions described in the if-clause are met, it guarantees the then-clause will happen. Test makers frequently attempt to hide conditional clauses with everyday language rather than using if-then statements. This is done by attaching an extreme verb or word like *guarantees*, *must*, *necessitates*, *only*, *unless*, or *whenever* to a clause.

While extreme language can appear in any type of question, there are some specific instances worth considering. For parallel reasoning and parallel flaw questions, extreme language can change the tone or meaning of arguments that would otherwise be similar. For inference and must-be-true questions, test takers should be wary of extreme language, which can stretch a reasonable inference too far. For example, there is a world of difference between an inference that something can be true and a statement that something is true. In contrast, extreme language is often helpful in strengthening-or-weakening questions because it does more work toward bolstering or undermining the argument. Similarly, extreme language might make for an ideal answer choice when you're trying to resolve a paradox because it is strong enough to definitively provide an explanation. However, all of these are merely general things to consider. Test makers often go against these rules of thumb to craft more difficult questions.

<u>Irrelevant Information and Similar Language</u>
Test makers include *irrelevant information* to obscure meaning with unnecessary details or information that's beyond the argument's scope. Correctly identifying the conclusion is the best way to determine if information is irrelevant. Any piece of information that doesn't support the conclusion is almost certainly irrelevant. Test takers should be especially cautious with strengthening-or-weakening questions. Because the correct answer will strengthen or weaken the argument, the incorrect answers must necessarily do the opposite or be irrelevant. Other types of questions that frequently feature irrelevant answer choices include questions asking for additional evidence, inferences, conclusions, principles, and points of disagreement.

Like irrelevant information, *similar language* is intended to confuse the test taker. In the answer choices, similar language is appealing because the connection attracts test takers' attention. Similar words or phrases might be lifted from the argument into an answer choice, but they might be used in a different way or be irrelevant to the task at hand. Furthermore, in inference-and-assumption questions, answer choices might mirror the argument, which means they are incorrect because an inference or assumption won't directly be included in the argument verbatim. Parallel reasoning questions also commonly use similar language to trick test takers. Remember that it's the logic that needs to be similar, not the language or superficial organization of the argument.

Consider the following example to understand how irrelevant information and similar language function in a strengthening question.

Environmentalist: Nuclear energy creates electricity through splitting an atom in a reactor. The split atom releases enough energy to heat water into steam, powering an electric turbine. The government needs to build more nuclear reactors because burning fossil fuels produces more carbon emissions, which are the leading cause of climate change. Nuclear energy is admittedly not a renewable energy source, and it does produce dangerous radioactive waste. However, renewable energy sources, like solar and wind energy, cannot possibly meet our country's current needs.

Which of the following statements, if true, would support the environmentalist's argument?

    a. Scientists disagree on whether carbon emissions are the leading cause of climate change.
    b. Renewable energy sources, like solar and wind energy, require batteries to store energy.
    c. Nuclear reactors are dangerous because an accident or attack could decimate an entire region.
    d. Deep geological disposal is a new safe and effective way to remove radioactive waste.
    e. American scientists achieved the first manmade nuclear chain reaction in 1942.
    This question was created by APEX Test Prep and is not an official LSAC question.

The first two sentences in the stimulus argument are irrelevant background information. The logistics of energy production doesn't impact the argument's conclusion that the government needs to build more nuclear reactors. Similarly, Choices *B* and *E* are irrelevant because they don't impact the conclusion or a supporting premise. Choices *A* and *B* use similar language as the argument, but they are also incorrect. Choice *A* would weaken the argument, and Choice *B* is irrelevant. Choice *C* would weaken the argument, so it's also incorrect. Choice *D* is correct because it counteracts a flaw admitted by the scientist, and thereby, strengthens the conclusion.

Appeals-to-Authority Fallacies
Anyone familiar with politics will be acquainted with appeals to authority. For example, when advocating for their fiscal agenda, politicians regularly cite economic studies. This appeal to authority leverages economists' subject matter expertise to bolster the politicians' arguments. However, in the context of the Logical Reasoning section, appeals to authority sometimes commit a logical fallacy by citing an inappropriate authority, usually due to a disconnect between the authority's expertise and the matter at hand. For example, if a stimulus argument describes a politician defending a tax cut, an appeal to the host of a news program would commit the appeal to authority fallacy, assuming there is no reason to believe the host is an economic expert. Unsurprisingly, the appeal to authority fallacy is most relevant in questions asking you to identify the flaw or flawed reasoning.

Test makers usually include an appeal to authority fallacy in two different ways. First, like the politician example above, the authority doesn't hold the relevant expertise. This variety is occasionally masked by naming an authority that is an expert but not for that subject matter. Consider the following argument:

Lawyer: Our criminal justice system is overwhelmed, bordering on collapse. Capable lawyers can handle somewhere between a dozen and two dozen active cases, but every prosecutor in our office is currently responsible for at least a hundred active cases. On top of that, we don't have enough judges or courtrooms to bring even half these cases to trial. As a result, we're being forced to emphasize expediency over justice. My best friend is a therapist, and she shares my concern that our justice system is doing a disservice to our community.

The lawyer's conclusion is that the criminal justice is in dire straits, inflicting harm on the community. To support this argument, the lawyer commits an appeal to authority fallacy by citing a therapist. While a therapist holds professional expertise in psychology, that expertise isn't relevant to analyzing a criminal justice system.

Second, an argument might properly cite authorities that have relevant expertise, but it can still be a fallacy when the conclusion arbitrarily argues that one authority is superior to another. Consider the following argument:

Dietician: Two of my colleagues, Dr. Li and Dr. Wallace, recently conducted studies that were published in a peer-reviewed scientific journal. Both studies involved participants who stopped eating carbohydrates. Dr. Li observed that all of the participants went into ketosis, and their bodies started burning fat for energy, resulting in rapid weight loss without any adverse effects. Dr. Wallace's study had similar findings in terms of participants' weight loss; however, she also found that some of the participants suffered from dehydration and other serious renal complications. So, whenever my patients want to lose weight, I tell them to stop eating carbohydrates.

The argument appeals to two appropriate authorities with subject matter expertise, but the dietician's conclusion ignores the adverse effects detected in Dr. Wallace's study. Because the conclusion is solely based on these two studies, there needs to be some explanation as to why the dietician isn't worried about her patients suffering from dehydration and other serious renal complications.

Hasty Generalizations

A *generalization* is an inference based on a part of a larger entity that's used to describe the larger entity. Generalizations can be useful because they act as an analytic shortcut. Instead of studying every individual member of a group, analyzing a representative cross-section of that group could deliver comparable results with less time and effort. However, generalizations should always be treated with skepticism because they require a sufficiently large body of evidence to be effective as a predictive tool. Generalizations are also heavily influenced by extreme language. When a generalization attempts to ascribe a characteristic to every member of the group, it can be refuted by a single contrarian case. As such, logically sound generalizations usually create some wiggle room with nonextreme language, such as *likely*, *most*, *tend to*, or *usually*.

When an inference lacks the evidence to support an overly broad inference, it's a *hasty generalization*. Hasty generalizations usually appear in questions asking you to identify the flaw or parallel flawed reasoning. Extrapolating from anecdotal experience is almost always a hasty generalization, especially when it's drawn from a single instance or example. Anecdotal evidence often leads to *cherry picking*, meaning that the evidence is selectively chosen to confirm a conclusion while ignoring contradictory evidence. Consider the following example:

Smoker: My grandfather smoked a pack of cigarettes every day, and he lived until he was one hundred years old. My parents each smoke two packs per day, and they're both still alive. So, I don't see the harm in smoking occasionally; I only ever smoke when I'm drinking.

The smoker concludes that smoking isn't harmful based on three people's anecdotal experience. This fails to consider that his grandfather and parents might be outliers, and he's assuming that he will also be an exception to the rule. Anecdotal evidence is almost never the basis for a logical generalization because it involves a limited sample size. When dealing with sample sizes, the larger, the better, because more data points create more representative results. Always be cautious with arguments that describe scientific experiments with limited sample sizes or speculate about the future based on short-term trends. In addition, look out for sample sizes that are asserted as if they are representative of a larger whole. Consider the following example:

A new high-tech mobile application pays people to participate in political polls as long as they are subscribed to a specific newspaper that's widely regarded as the nation's least partisan publication. The application's most recent poll found that nine out of ten voters favor the Blue Party's presidential candidate. Therefore, the Blue Party's candidate will win the presidential election.

Although nine out of ten voters favor the Blue Party's candidate, only a tiny fraction of the total population was polled. To participate, someone would need to own a mobile phone, subscribe to a specific newspaper, and download the mobile application. In other words, it's only telling us who technologically savvy, nonpartisan voters favor in the election, so using this poll to infer how the entire electorate will vote is a hasty generalization.

Basic Concepts

Conditional Statements

Conditional statements are among the most frequently tested logical concepts in the Logical Reasoning section. Some questions, like *syllogisms*, which test deductive reasoning, are nearly impossible to answer without understanding how conditional statements function. Conditional statements also make other questions much easier to answer, such as inference and must-be-true questions. The most recognizable conditional statements appear in the form of if-then clauses. Consider the following example:

If test takers score at least 160 on the LSAT, then they will be admitted into law school.

The if-clause is referred to as the *hypothesis*, and the then-clause is the *conclusion*. For conditional statements, the if-clause is always a sufficient condition to trigger the conclusion. So, in the example above, achieving a score of at least 160 guarantees that test taker will be admitted to law school. According to this conditional statement's internal logic, there is no scenario where someone scores 160 or more and doesn't get admitted into law school. To make the analysis easier, most people try to translate conditional statements into an abbreviated form, especially when there are multiple conditional statements in play. The conditional statement above could be abbreviated as: $\geq 160 \rightarrow L$.

An arrow is usually used to mark the divide between the two clauses. In other words, you replace "then" with an arrow. The abbreviations you choose don't matter as long as you understand what they mean, and you use them consistently. In this example, ≥ 160 means "greater than or equal to 160" on the LSAT, and L means "admitted into law school." A good rule of thumb is to make the abbreviations as short as possible without sacrificing comprehension. Let's consider the difference between two abbreviations:

$\geq 160 \rightarrow L$

Score at least 160 $\rightarrow$ Admitted into law school

The second example is abbreviated when compared to the original if-then statement, but it's considerably longer than the other abbreviated example. Being concise saves time, and it's also important for staying consistent. When there are a handful of conditional statements, a single abbreviation should be used for every clause that carries a common meaning.

You need to know three fundamental characteristics about conditional statements. First, flipping a conditional statement to get its converse doesn't preserve the original statement's logical validity. Let's take the converse of our example:

If test takers are admitted into law school, then they scored at least 160 on the LSAT.

This converse of the original conditional statement isn't necessarily true. Based on the original conditional statement, scoring 160 is a sufficient condition. In other words, whoever scores at least 160 will be admitted to law school. However, this isn't a necessary condition, so not everyone who gets into law school will have scored at least 160. Those students might have satisfied a different sufficient condition, like a high GPA, to get into law school.

Second, the inverse of a conditional statement is achieved by negating both sides of the original conditional statement. Let's take the inverse of our example:

If test takers do not score at least 160 on the LSAT, then they will not be admitted into law school.

The inverse doesn't necessarily follow logically from the original conditional statement. Like the converse, the inverse fails because it is turning a sufficient condition into a necessary condition.

Unlike the converse and inverse, the *contrapositive* always has the same truth value as the original conditional statement. The contrapositive can be found by inverting the converse. Let's take the contrapositive of our example:

If test takers are not admitted into law school, then they did not score at least 160 on the LSAT.

This has the same truth value as the original conditional statement, as it maintains the same sufficient condition. Because everybody who scores at least 160 gets admitted into law school, then it must be true that nobody who's not admitted scored at least 160.

So, for the Logical Reasoning section, it's usually worthwhile to take the contrapositive of a conditional statement because we know it must be true if the original conditional statement is true. The contrapositive might fill a missing link between other conditionals that wouldn't otherwise be clear. Similarly, the converse and inverse of conditional statements should be treated with caution because they don't necessarily have the same truth values as the original conditional statement.

Reasonableness
In the Logical Reasoning section, as well as in the rest of the LSAT, everything must be contained within the information that's provided. If something isn't explicitly present in a question, then it's not part of that argument. In other words, your prior knowledge about the substantive topics included in the arguments is irrelevant. Let's say you majored in American history, and you come across the following question:

The Confederate States of America seceded over states' rights. The Confederacy's chief export was cotton, and American historians believe that a series of cotton tariffs harmed the Confederacy. In addition, one Confederate state had more indentured servants than slaves. As such, slavery couldn't have been the primary reason why the Confederacy seceded.

The argument above is most vulnerable to criticism on the grounds that:

    a. it commits a logical fallacy by appealing to an inappropriate authority.
    b. it offers a red herring instead of supporting the argument.
    c. it makes a hasty generalization based on insufficient evidence.
    d. it reaches its conclusion by begging the question.
    e. it draws a false distinction between states' rights and slavery.
    This question was created by APEX Test Prep and is not an official LSAC question.

As an American history major, you know that the South seceded primarily over the right to own slaves. Although Choice *E* hints at this mistake, this answer choice relies on outside information. So, Choice *C* is the superior answer because it addresses a mistake committed within the stated argument. The argument claims that one state had more indentured servants than slaves, but what about the other states? This is a hasty generalization because the argument is drawing a conclusion about the whole based on a single part. The argument does appeal to authority, but it's an appropriate authority, so Choice *A* is incorrect. The argument doesn't offer a red herring or beg the question, so Choices *B* and *D* are also incorrect'

Test makers will try to lure you into injecting your outside knowledge into the argument by preying on your personal biases, judgments, and values. Remember that arguments in the Logical Reasoning section do not need to be ethical, factual, logical, objective, rational, or something a reasonable person would likely agree with. Even when the argument reaches an unreasonable conclusion, like defending corruption as being essential to public service, always limit your analysis to the argument's internal logic.

Incomplete and Unknown Arguments

The Logical Reasoning section contains two different types of faulty argumentation—incomplete arguments and unknown arguments. *Incomplete arguments* lack an essential element. As described above, those essential elements are a conclusion and premises supporting that conclusion. An unstated conclusion might be implied or not present at all. Consider the following example of an incomplete argument that lacks a conclusion:

Anyone who studies for the LSAT for at least five hours per day will be able to attend whatever law school they want. Todd has been studying for ten hours every day.

The logical conclusion is that Todd will be able to attend whatever law school he wants, but that's not what the argument says. As such, it's an incomplete argument. Test takers primarily omit conclusions for two reasons. First, people have an innate impulse to jump to conclusions when they're provided with evidence. The brain naturally attempts to organize information around a conclusion. As such, test takers should be wary of inserting their own conclusion into an incomplete argument. Second, several types of questions either explicitly or implicitly ask you to identify a conclusion. For example, the correct answer to must-be-true, main point, and primary purpose questions are often interchangeable with what the conclusion would be if it were stated.

An incomplete argument that lacks premises will have insufficient or no evidence in support of its conclusion. If some evidence is provided, it might be insufficient when it's not persuasive or relies on assumptions. Some assumptions are required to complete an argument because they tie two or more premises together. Logical Reasoning arguments are rarely composed of a solitary conclusion without any evidence at all; rather, the evidence provided will be irrelevant, which means it doesn't support the conclusion. Assumptions and irrelevant evidence are both discussed in greater detail in the following sections. Consider the following example of an incomplete argument that lacks proper premises:

Social media is causing a mental health crisis amongst young people. Computers and phones are exorbitantly expensive, and they become obsolete within a few years.

This is an incomplete argument because the premises (second sentence) don't support the conclusion (first sentence). Devices' price and durability aren't directly related to a mental health crisis. Alternatively, if those premises are relevant, the argument is incomplete because it's missing a dependent assumption, like the lack of access to social media being known to cause anxiety.

Unknown arguments lack a conclusion, and it's often difficult to determine whether what's presented is meant to be an argument. Fact sets are an example of an unknown argument. Consider the following example of an unknown argument:

The hotel has 200 rooms. Every room costs $100 per night, and the pet fee is $20. The hotel is located on Main Street.

This is a description, not an argument. Not only is there no explicit conclusion, no reasonable conclusion could possibly be drawn from this set of facts. So, like incomplete arguments without a conclusion, test takers should be careful not to add their own conclusion. Unknown arguments are relatively rare, but they do occasionally pop up in questions asking you to identify a conclusion, main point, or primary purpose.

Patterns of Reasoning

One of the question types in the Logical Reasoning section of the LSAT exam will ask about patterns of reasoning. Patterns of reasoning involve deconstructing an argument and putting general terms to each of the steps involved. Then, it is up to the test taker to apply those general terms to another specific argument. The following is an example of a question stem involving patterns of reasoning:

> Hernandez is the best pitcher in the league. He plays for the Robins who are playing the Billie Goats, the worst team in the league. Since Hernandez is the starting pitcher for tonight's game, the Robins will win.

The pattern of flawed reasoning in which one of the following flawed arguments is most similar to that in the argument above?

a. Ms. Ethel bakes the best apple pies in Johnson County. She entered the annual pie contest at the Johnson County Fair. Ms. Ethel has been making pies since before any of the other contestants were born; therefore, she will win the contest.
b. To boost productivity, the supervisor at the Widget Factory has challenged Assembly Line A and Assembly Line B to see who can produce more widgets in the next three hours. Assembly Line A is led by Janelle, the fastest widget maker in the company, and Assembly Line B is less experienced than A. Assembly Line A will win.
c. Andrew is the smartest kid in the school district. He and his team have an upcoming math competition, against the school with the lowest average GPA in the district. Andrew's team will win.
d. TechWorks computers have the fastest processors on the market in them. Computerly computers have the slowest processors on the market in them. Assuming the same Internet speed, a TechWorks computer will download and upload files faster than a Computerly computer.
e. Mark has 10 years of experience as a salesman at the surf shop, while other employees are recent hires. Mark will win Employee of the Year.
This question was created by APEX Test Prep and is not an official LSAC question.

Let's find out what the logical structure of this argument is. For visual learners, it may help to write out or draw a logical sequence of statements. For now, we can see the following:

> Hernandez is the best.
> Hernandez is a part of the Robins.
> The team (Billie Goats) they are playing is the worst.
> Hernandez's team (Robins) will beat the Billie Goats.

We can abbreviate it like this:

> H is best
> H is a part of R
> BG is worst
> R will beat BG

It's important to note that H is a component of R. Most of the answer choices fail to have that aspect to them.

Again, this is flawed reasoning. H being the best and BG being the worst do not ensure that R will beat BG. Now, let's evaluate the answer choices to find flawed reasoning that is structured the same way.

Choice A
In this choice, Ms. Ethel is the best but is not part of a larger group like Hernandez is. Additionally, she has many opponents in this scenario, whereas R just had one.

Choice B
This choice has the following construction:

> J is Best
> J is a part of A
> B is less experienced
> A will beat B

This is very similar construction, but different than the original one. Whereas the Billie Goats were the worst team, Assembly Line B is just less experienced, not necessarily the worst.

Choice C
This choice is correct. It is flawed in the same way that the original scenario is flawed, such that a strong "parallel" exists between the two.

> Andrew is the smartest.
> Andrew is part of a team.
> The school they are competing against scores the lowest.
> Andrew's school will beat the other school.

The argument is structured the same as the one about the baseball team. Additionally, the reasoning is flawed because the factors given do not guarantee a certain outcome.

Choice D
This option is close to having the correct construction:

> Processor in TechWorks is the fastest
> Processor in Computerly is the slowest
> TechWorks will beat Computerly.

Remember that the flawed reasoning in the original scenario was based on a player (or component) of one team being the best and the opposing team being the worst.

Here, it is saying the component of one computer is the best and the *component* of the other computer is the worst. To be parallel, it would have to say that the Computerly computer as a whole is the slowest on the market, not just a component of it.

Choice E
Like Choice *A*, this scenario fails to include an individual or object being a component of a larger organization that is competing. While Mark is an employee of the surf shop, the surf shop is not the one competing. Rather, he's competing against the other employees for the Employee of the Year award.

Drawing Well-Supported Conclusions
The conclusion question types in the Logical Reasoning section presents evidence within the stimulus and asks test takers to draw a conclusion from that evidence. Some of the conclusion question types will ask what test takers can "infer," "imply," or "conclude" from the given information. Other language used in conclusion questions might consist of the following:

- Must also be true
- Provide the most support for
- Which one of the following conclusions
- Most strongly supported by
- Properly inferred

Making inferences and drawing conclusions involve skills that are quite similar: both require readers to fill in information the test writer has omitted. To make an inference or draw a conclusion about the text, test takers should observe all facts and arguments the test writer has presented. The best way to understand ways to drawing well-supported conclusions is by practice. Let's take a look at the following example:

Nutritionist: More and more bodybuilders each year turn to whey protein as a source for their supplement intake to repair muscle tissue after working out. More and more studies are showing that using whey as a source of protein is linked to prostate cancer in men. Bodybuilders who use whey protein may consider switching to a plant-based protein source in order to avoid developing the negative effects that come with whey protein consumption.

Which of the following most accurately expresses the conclusion of the nutritionist's argument?

> a. Whey protein is an excellent way to repair muscles after a workout.
> b. Bodybuilders should switch from whey to a plant-based protein.
> c. Whey protein causes every single instance of prostate cancer in men.
> d. We still don't know the causes of prostate cancer in men.
> e. It's possible that bodybuilding may cause prostate cancer.
> *This question was created by APEX Test Prep and is not an official LSAC question.*

The correct answer choice is *B*: bodybuilders should switch from whey to a plant-based protein. We can gather this from the entirety of the passage, as it begins with what kind of protein bodybuilders consume, the dangers of that protein, and what kind of protein to switch to. Choice *A* is incorrect; this is the opposite of what the passage states. When reading through answer choices, it's important to look for choices that include the words "every," "always," or "all." In many instances, absolute answer choices will not be the correct answer. This example is shown in Choice *C*; the passage does not state that whey protein causes "every single instance" of prostate cancer in men, only that it is *linked* to prostate cancer in men. Choice *D* is incorrect; although the nutritionist doesn't list all the causes of prostate cancer in men, the nutritionist does not conclude that we don't know the causes of prostate cancer in men either. Finally, Choice *E* is incorrect. This answer choice makes a jump from bodybuilding to prostate cancer, which is incorrect. The passage states that bodybuilders consume more whey protein, which is linked to cancer, not that bodybuilding *itself* causes cancer.

The key to drawing well-supported conclusions is to read the question stem in its entirety a few times over and then paraphrase the passage in your own words. Once you do this, you will get an idea of the passage's conclusion before you are confused by all the different answer choices. Remember that drawing a conclusion is different than making an assumption. With drawing a conclusion, we are relying solely on the passage for facts to come to our conclusion. Making an assumption goes beyond the facts of the passage, so be careful of answer choices depicting assumptions instead of passage-based conclusions.

Common Question Types

Main Point/Primary Purpose
Main point and primary purpose questions are both relatively simple. For *main point* questions, ask yourself what the author is hoping to convey with the argument. Oftentimes the conclusion is interchangeable with an argument's main point. Similarly, for *primary purpose* questions, ask yourself why the author is making this argument and whom it seems to be addressing. Although the argument's target audience is usually left unstated, the author's tone and style are often helpful hints. For example, an argument might be trying to summarize, persuade, or reconcile conflicting views.

Let's look at an example of a main point and primary purpose question. Use the following argument to answer both questions.

Historian: Prohibition is almost always portrayed as an overreaction, the product of mass hysteria and religious extremism. However, Prohibition was an understandable policy goal when placed in historical context. First, the United States was experiencing unprecedented socioeconomic shifts, including mass immigration, industrialization, and urbanization. Second, societal unrest directly resulted in a massive increase to per capita alcohol consumption, leading to more public corruption, unemployment, and the dissolution of families. Third, women could not vote and were largely barred from meaningful work, so if their husbands were violent drunkards, there was little they could do.

Which of the following is the main point of the passage?

   a. Prohibition occurred after the United States experienced unprecedented socioeconomic shifts.
   b. Prohibition was the product of mass hysteria, religious extremism, and societal unrest.
   c. Women were treated unfairly prior to the criminalization of alcohol.
   d. Alcohol consumption is related to corruption, unemployment, and the dissolution of families.
   e. Historical context illustrates why Prohibition was rational in the moment.
   This question was created by APEX Test Prep and is not an official LSAC question.

Which of the following is the passage's primary purpose?

    a. To reconcile opposing views on how Prohibition is portrayed in the mainstream media
    b. To summarize how Prohibition successfully banned the sale of alcohol
    c. To challenge a popular view based on its failure to consider historical context
    d. To argue that Prohibition was the correct response to societal unrest in hindsight
    e. To attack people who think Prohibition was the product of mass hysteria and religious extremism
    This question was created by APEX Test Prep and is not an official LSAC question.

The historian's main point is that historical context disproves the popular characterization of Prohibition. Rather than a hysterical overreaction, the historian argues that Prohibition was a rational policy goal at that moment in time. Thus, Choice *E* is the correct answer. Choices *A*, *C*, and *D* merely restate the historian's premises about historical context, so they are all incorrect. Choice *B* is incorrect because it contradicts the historian's main point.

The historian's primary purpose is to challenge the popular portrayal of Prohibition as the product of mass hysteria and religious extremism, and the argument does so by providing historical context to show why Prohibition was understandable. Thus, Choice *C* is the correct answer. Choice *A* is incorrect because the historian isn't reconciling the two views. The historian is refuting the popular portrayal. The historian's argument does not explain how Prohibition banned alcohol or discuss whether it was successful, so Choice *B* is incorrect. Choice *D* is incorrect because it goes too far. We only know that the historian thinks Prohibition was understandable, not that it was correct in hindsight. Choice *E* is incorrect because it doesn't match the historian's tone. The historian is trying to correct a misconception, not attack people who hold a mistaken belief.

Reasoning by Analogy
Analogy questions in the Logical Reasoning section of the LSAT exam are very common. In its most basic definition, an *analogy* is a comparison between two things. Lawyers use reasoning by analogy frequently in their professional careers in order to compare past successful cases with present cases they are trying to argue. For analogy questions, there are several specific question types you will run into:

Flawed Reasoning
For analogies in flawed reasoning questions, many people make the mistake of assuming that the two things being compared *are alike in every respect*. If they are not, it is flawed reasoning by analogy.

Let's look at an example at a faulty analogy in a flawed reasoning question:

Mary Oliver is a great poet, and she practices writing every single day. Therefore, if I practice writing every single day, I will be a great poet.

The example above is flawed because it assumes that Mary Oliver and I are the same in every respect. Perhaps she received a better education than me, and that is why she is a great poet. Or maybe her father was a poet and taught her everything she needed to know to be a great poet. The possibilities are endless as to why this analogy does not work out.

Necessary Assumption
We will talk in depth about necessary assumption later, but for the sake of necessary assumption dealing with analogy, let's use the same example above. A necessary assumption means that at least one thing

must be required in order for the argument to be true. Here is a proper answer to a necessary assumption question dealing with analogy:

Mary Oliver practices writing, and her practice causes her to become a stronger writer. Therefore, if I practice writing every day, I will become a stronger writer.

What is an assumption on which this argument relies?

All humans that practice writing will get better due to the neurological structure of the brain and how the brain responds to that practice.

For necessary assumption, we want to look at how the two entities are similar *in at least one aspect*. We see here that, at the very least, Mary Oliver and I are both human, and that our brains will respond similarly to practice, leading to stronger writing.

Sufficient Assumption

Again, we will go into more depth on sufficient assumption questions later, but let's look at these types of questions dealing with analogies. For a sufficient assumption, we want the two entities to be alike *in all related respects*.

Mary Oliver practices writing, and her practice causes her to become a stronger writer. Therefore, if I practice writing every day, I will become a stronger writer.

Which of the following, if assumed, allows the conclusion to be drawn properly?

Every human responds in the same way when they practice writing.

Whether this is true in real life or not, we have a valid argument with this sufficient assumption question. Analogies in the sufficient assumption context tell us that Mary Oliver and I are the same in every way when we practice writing; therefore, my assertion to become a stronger writer is totally valid.

Inferences

Inference questions require test takers to read between the lines. The correct answer will be something that the argument is implying. Some questions will directly ask what can be properly inferred from the argument, but others will ask for a statement supported by the argument. Alternatively, the question could ask for a statement the author would agree with. Consider the following statement:

> Jose had to stay late at work again, so he couldn't go to the gym.

Multiple inferences can be drawn from this statement. Because Jose needed to stay at work, we know that he is employed, and the fact that he needed to stay late *again* creates an inference that his job is demanding. Likewise, the second clause leads to the inference that Jose is physically active and likely has a gym membership. Arguments will have more complex inferences than statements, but the general principle is the same.

Now let's look at an inference question:

Dentist: Flossing is critical for dental health. My patients who floss regularly need to schedule only one visit per year, and those who floss irregularly need to schedule at least three visits per year. I refuse to see patients who never floss because I don't specialize in dental surgery.

The argument most strongly supports which of the following statements?

    a. Flossing improves dental health more than regularly brushing teeth.
    b. People don't need to floss if they visit the dentist at least three times per year.
    c. Some people who floss regularly will require dental surgery.
    d. Some people who floss irregularly will require dental surgery.
    e. People who don't floss will likely require dental surgery.
    This question was created by APEX Test Prep and is not an official LSAC question.

Choice *E* is the correct answer. The dentist won't see patients who never floss because the dentist doesn't specialize in dental surgery, so it can be inferred that people who don't floss will likely require dental surgery. Otherwise it wouldn't make sense that the dentist would refuse to see patients who don't floss. Choices *C* and *D* could be true, but they are less strongly supported than Choice *E*. Choices *A* and *B* aren't at all supported by the argument, so they are also incorrect.

Except Type of New Information Questions

Test makers occasionally include questions with EXCEPT or NOT written in capital letters to emphasize that you're being asked to identify the answer choice that's unlike the others. This usually occurs with question types that ask how new information would impact the argument, like paradox, principle, strengthen, and weaken questions. You should always read questions with extreme care, but this is particularly important in questions asking for an exception. If you miss the EXCEPT or NOT, then you'll almost certainly get the answer wrong.

The good news is that these types of questions aren't any more difficult than their normal counterparts as long as you realize what's being asked. If anything, most students find these to be among the easiest questions in the Logical Reasoning section. When a question is written with EXCEPT or NOT, the correct answer will always either be irrelevant to the argument or have the opposite effect on the argument as compared to the other four answer choices.

Let's look at an example of a question asking for an exception:

Investing in public transportation is the best way to combat climate change. The United States currently lags behind other industrialized countries when it comes to accessible public transportation, and Americans drive the highest number of miles per capita by a significant margin. In addition, the developing world has totally inadequate public transportation networks. So, America needs to take immediate action before climate change destabilizes the entire world.

Each of the following, if true, strengthens the argument EXCEPT:

    a. Other industrialized countries enjoy greater access to renewable energy resources.
    b. Driving burns the most fossil fuels, which causes climate change.
    c. The United States is a world leader, and developing countries always follow the world leader.
    d. Public transportation networks can be built quickly and efficiently.
    e. Global destabilization would threaten American interests.
    This question was created by APEX Test Prep and is not an official LSAC question.

Because this is an EXCEPT question, all of the incorrect answer choices will strengthen the argument, and the correct answer will either weaken or be irrelevant to the argument. The argument's conclusion is that the United States needs to invest in public transportation to combat climate change. Choice *B* is incorrect it supports the United States being a leading contributor to climate change. Choice *C* is incorrect because if America is a world leader that developing countries will follow, then developing countries will also improve their inadequate public transportation networks. If public transportations can be built quickly and efficiently, then its investment will have an immediate effect, so Choice *D* is incorrect. Choice *E* is incorrect because if climate change causes global destabilization that threatens American interests, then the United States should combat climate change by investing in public transportation. Other industrialized countries' access to renewable resources isn't directly related to the argument's conclusion; rather, it's merely providing background information, so Choice *A* is the correct answer.

Flawed Reasoning

Flawed reasoning questions are why it's generally a good idea to read the question before the stimulus argument. Some Logical Reasoning arguments are obviously flawed, but many appear quite logical. If you know the argument is flawed beforehand, you can direct your time and energy into spotting the flaw from the outset. Once you spot the flaw, try to paraphrase it before reading the answer choices. However, if you can't figure out what is wrong with the argument, try to weaken the argument. Oftentimes an argument's flaw is its greatest weakness, so even if you don't realize it's a logical flaw, you might pick up on that weakness anyway.

Flawed reasoning questions contain some of the trickiest answer choices because some will accurately describe the argument's reasoning. Not everything in a flawed argument is illogical, so always make sure the answer you choose directly addresses the flaw.

Let's look at an example of a flawed reasoning question:

Elizabeth's pediatrician wants to give her baby three vaccines at an upcoming appointment. The pediatrician claims the vaccines will protect her baby against polio, measles, and chickenpox. However, Elizabeth is concerned. She recently attended a support group for new mothers, and all of the attendees' children developed autism after they were vaccinated. Elizabeth trusts her pediatrician's judgment, but she still wants to postpone the vaccines until she has time to do more research.

Which one of the following is a flaw in the argument's reasoning?

    a. The pediatrician's medical advice is based on a fallacious appeal to authority.
    b. The pediatrician is appealing to emotion to convince Elizabeth to vaccinate her baby.
    c. Elizabeth relies on an ad hominem attack to undermine the pediatrician's judgment.
    d. Elizabeth engages in circular reasoning to justify postponing the vaccinations.
    e. Elizabeth is drawing her conclusion based on a hasty generalization.
    This question was created by APEX Test Prep and is not an official LSAC question.

Elizabeth trusts her pediatrician's judgment, but she's postponing the vaccines based on a hasty generalization she heard at the support group. Although all of the attendees' children developed autism after their vaccinations, that doesn't necessarily mean vaccination causes autism. Those children are a tiny fraction of all the children who receive vaccinations. Thus, Choice *E* is the correct answer. The pediatrician's medical advice is based on her expertise, which isn't a fallacious appeal to authority, so Choice *A* is incorrect. Likewise, the pediatrician doesn't make an appeal to emotion, so Choice *B* is incorrect. Elizabeth doesn't attack the doctor's character or engage in circular reasoning; thus, Choices *C* and *D* are also incorrect.

Parallel Reasoning

Test takers generally struggle with parallel reasoning questions due to the amount of work they require. Like other question types, *parallel reasoning* questions include a stimulus argument, but they also include arguments as answer choices. This means test takers need to analyze six different arguments to find the correct answer. Consequently, if you're running short on time, it's generally advisable to complete other questions before returning to the remaining parallel reasoning questions.

The important thing to remember when answering parallel reasoning questions is that only the logical reasoning needs to be the same. Test makers will use similar language, substance, and organization to distract you from the arguments' internal logic. Consequently, you should break down each argument into premises, assumptions, flaws, conditional statements, subconclusions, and conclusions wherever relevant. When an answer choice argument doesn't contain the same elements or deploys them differently compared to the stimulus argument, it's likely incorrect.

Another variety of parallel reasoning question includes flaws in the stimulus argument and answer choices. Despite their superficial differences, parallel flawed reasoning questions are identical to what's described above except the correct answer will have the same flaw as the argument. Just as how normal parallel reasoning questions will have answer choices with different types of logical arguments, test makers will include other flawed arguments in the incorrect answer choices. As such, it's important to know and be able to distinguish between common logical flaws, which are discussed in detail below.

Let's look at an example of a flawed parallel reasoning question:

Tina is a big Giants fan. She thinks the Giants are the best team in football because no other team can outplay them.

Which of the following contains a flaw that most closely parallels the flaw contained in the argument above?

    a. Joseph is a big Nirvana fan. He thinks Nirvana's Kurt Cobain and Dave Grohl were the most talented guitarist and drummer combo ever featured in the same band.
    b. You need to save money for retirement because you can't retire without adequate savings.
    c. We need to go see this pop-up art show. My friend Jonny is a world-class musician, and he highly recommends it.
    d. Pizza is the best food in the world. Nine out of ten kids in my middle school class chose pizza as their favorite food.
    e. I didn't get the job. I must either have been overqualified or underqualified for the position.
    This question was created by APEX Test Prep and is not an official LSAC question.

The stimulus argument engages in circular reasoning. Tina is essentially arguing that the Giants are the best team because the Giants are the best team. Choice *B* contains the same flaw. That argument says you need to save for retirement because you can't retire without saving. Both are circular arguments because the premises are merely restating the assumed conclusion. None of the other answer choices includes circular reasoning, so Choice *B* is the correct answer. Choice *A* is superficially similar to the stimulus argument, but its logic is quite different. Joseph is arguing that he's a fan of Nirvana because Kurt Cobain and Dave Grohl were supremely talented musicians. There is more substance to Joseph's argument than what appears in the stimulus argument. Choice *C* is incorrect because it commits a fallacious appeal to authority. Choice *D* is incorrect because it makes a hasty generalization. Choice *E* is incorrect because it features a false choice error. There could be many reasons the job was not secured. Additionally, it doesn't follow the format or reasoning of the stimulus.

Recognizing Misunderstandings or Points of Disagreement

On the LSAT, some question stems will have two separate passages addressing a similar topic. Both passages will be spoken by someone like a scientist, politician, or doctor, or it might even just be someone's last name, like "Rodriguez" or "Powell." The two passages are meant to disagree with or misunderstand each other. The question will usually ask a "point at issue" between the two speakers, or how the two speakers disagree in the passages. The answer explanations will try to throw in choices that relate to the topic but ones the speakers do not have opinions on. Watch out for these, as they are only meant to confuse you. Regarding the choices, ask yourself, first and foremost, does either speaker have an opinion on this statement? And if no opinion is expressed in the original passage, mark the answer as incorrect. Let's look at an example of a Point at Issue question:

Jones: Our company's decision to change driving routes may have been detrimental to the company. The new route is longer by half an hour, which cuts down the efficiency of when the goods get delivered, which, in turn, makes us lose money.

Martinez: The newer, updated route was the best decision. The old route had safety hazards for truck drivers. The newer route will cut down on accidents, which will make up for the cost of delivering the goods later.

A point of issue between Jones and Martinez is whether

      a. the new driving route will save the company money.
      b. the old driving route is safer than the new driving route.
      c. the company will go bankrupt due to this change in route.
      d. the shipment will make it on time via the new route.
      e. the goods are too expensive and should be lowered.
      This question was created by APEX Test Prep and is not an official LSAC question.

The correct answer choice is *A*. Jones and Martinez disagree over whether the new driving route will save the company money. Choice *B* is incorrect; although Martinez admits that the new route is safer than the old route, Jones has no opinion on safety, which makes this choice incorrect. Choice *C* is incorrect; neither of the speakers mention the company's potential to go bankrupt. In Choice *D*, Jones is worried about shipments making it on time, but Martinez is not concerned with time here; Martinez is more concerned with safety. Finally, Choice *E* is incorrect; neither speaker worries about the price of the goods. When reading the answer choices, make sure each speaker has an opinion concerning the one you choose. Here, we see both speakers mention money saved, so Choice *A* is the correct answer choice.

Determining How Additional Evidence Affects an Argument

Questions seeking evidence that most undermines or weakens the argument require test takers to read the stated premises in the argument and ask themselves what must be assumed true, but is not explicitly stated in the provided premises, in order for the argument to jump to its conclusion. The correct answer choice most directly contradicts, rules out, or refutes the identified unstated assumption or missing link. Questions seeking evidence that most strengthens or supports the argument require a similar approach with test takers considering the same question as they read the argument. Once the assumption is identified, they should review the answer choices for the one that most directly affirms or presents that missing link.

First, let's take a look at a weakening question below:

Samson owns and manages an orchard and likes to track the growth patterns of his trees. The mature trees have averaged 7" of upward growth the last three years. He plans to switch to a new fertilizer next year. In testing it for one year on a trial set of trees in his orchard, the trees grew an average of 2" higher than the trees that were on the old fertilizer. Because of that, he is predicting that next year's growth for his trees with be 9":

Samson's argument would be most weakened by which one of the following, if that statement were true?
  a. The next year is a Leap Year, so the trees will have one day longer to grow.
  b. The fertilizer has a larger effect the first year it is used than it does in subsequent years.
  c. Samson is entering semi-retirement in which one of his employees will be taking on more of the duties of orchard management.
  d. The town where the orchard is located has received higher than average rainfall for the last three years.
  e. Samson is also planting blueberry bushes.
  This question was created by APEX Test Prep and is not an official LSAC question.

The correct answer is Choice *D*. Rainfall generally has a positive correlation with plant growth. Since the rainfall has been higher than average, it is likely that the trees grew more than they would under normal conditions. For a prediction, average rainfall should be assumed, which means that the trees will likely grow less than 9". While one extra day in the year would technically have some effect (Choice *A*), it would be too miniscule to matter. Choice *B* is irrelevant, because the fertilizer was only tested for one year on the test trees and this will be the first year is it used on the orchard as a whole. Choice *C* could certainly have an effect as the orchard will be under different care. However, the effect on growth is unknown compared to Choice *D*. Choice *E* is incorrect, because blueberry bushes should not have any direct effect on the growth of the trees.

The following is an example of a strengthening argument:

Sandblast is a Norwegian company that makes computers, and Sandblast computers can run for twenty-four hours without having to charge them. Iberion is also a Norwegian company that makes computers; therefore, Iberion computers should also run for twenty-four hours without having to charge them.

The author's argument would be best supported by which one of the following, if that statement were true?

  a. Swedish computers also have the same amount of battery life as Norwegian computers.
  b. All Norwegian computer companies use the same types of batteries in their computers.
  c. The Iberion company focuses on manufacturing computers used specifically for commercial purposes.
  d. Iberion has been making computers for approximately fifteen years.
  e. All Norwegian computer companies have excellent customer service reviews.
  This question was created by APEX Test Prep and is not an official LSAC question.

First, let's look at the premise and the conclusion. The premise states that Sandblast computers are Norwegian and can run for twenty-four hours on battery and that Iberion computers are also Norwegian. Therefore, Iberion computers should also run for twenty-four hours on battery. Choice *B* is the correct answer because it displays the *similarities* between Sandblast and Iberion: they are both Norwegian and therefore both use the same batteries in their computers. Choices that have irrelevant information are

Choices *A*, *D*, and *E*. Choice *C* tells us what the Iberion company focuses on; however, we do not receive information on how this compares to Sandblast computers. Therefore, Choice *B* is the correct answer. If Norwegian companies put the same batteries in all of their computers, then it is likely that Sandblast computers and Iberion computers will run on battery power for a similar amount of time.

Detecting Assumptions Made by Particular Arguments
In the questions directly seeking an unstated assumption, test takers should read the stated premises in the argument and ask themselves what must be assumed true—but that is not explicitly stated in the provided premises—in order for the argument to jump to its conclusion. The correct answer choice will best present that missing link. Here's what assumption questions look like:

- Which of the following, if true, enables the conclusion to be properly drawn?
- The conclusion above is properly drawn if which of the following is assumed?
- The conclusion above follows logically if which one of the following is assumed?
- The argument makes which one of the following assumptions?
- Which of the following is an assumption upon which the argument relies?

Necessary Assumption
Some questions will deal with necessary assumptions, and some questions will deal with sufficient assumptions. Necessary assumptions are assumptions that have to be true in order for the conclusion to hold up. Remember that the basic argument structure goes from premise to conclusion. A necessary assumption is a statement in the middle of the premise and conclusion that is needed in order for the argument to not fall apart. Really, a necessary assumption is an unstated premise in the argument. Necessary assumption questions will use the words "required," "depends," or "relies." Let's look at a necessary assumption example:

Alachua County in Florida has reported no traces of manatees in their river systems from their recent surveys. If there were any manatees present, the surveys would have definitely detected them. Because no manatees were detected, we must conclude that they are extinct.

What is an assumption on which this argument relies?

 a. Manatees have been on the verge of extinction before, in the 1990s.
 b. The water this year in the river system has been colder than usual.
 c. Manatees do not exist anywhere outside of the Alachua County river system.
 d. Surveys are becoming more and more accurate for environmental research.
 e. Alachua County has also been seeing a decline in gators in the rivers.
 This question was created by APEX Test Prep and is not an official LSAC question.

Choice *C* is the correct answer choice. Again, a necessary assumption is an unstated premise on which the argument relies. One way to tell if you are choosing the right answer is to negate the answer choice. If we negated the answer choice and the conclusion falls apart, we have chosen the correct answer. Let's negate it: Manatees *do* exist outside of the Alachua County river system. Thus, our argument falls apart because that means that manatees are in fact *not* extinct. This argument is relying on the fact that manatees *do not* exist outside of the Alachua County river system, thus it is a necessary assumption.

Just for fun, let's negate the rest of the answer choices and see if our argument is destroyed. Choice *A*: If we see manatees have *not* been on the verge of extinction before, would that change the fact that they are on the verge of extinction now? Nope. Choice *B*: The water this year in the river systems has *not* been colder than usual. This does not destroy our conclusion that manatees are extinct. Choice *D*: Surveys are *not* becoming more and more accurate for environmental research. No, this does not destroy our argument, although it does wobble it a little. But for necessary assumption, remember that it must obliterate our conclusion, which *D* does not do. Choice *E:* Alachua County has *not* been seeing a decline in gators in the river. This has nothing to do with manatees, so we can mark it as incorrect.

Sufficient Assumption
Sufficient assumption questions are also known as "justify" questions on the LSAT, although the question stem will rarely contain the word "justify." Sufficient assumption stems present an argument that is not a whole argument. For sufficient assumption questions, we want to look for an answer choice with information that validates the argument. Remember how necessary assumption questions will contain the words "depends," "relies," and "requires"? Sufficient assumption questions will look like the following, often containing words like "Follows logically if . . . assumed," "Properly inferred if . . . assumed," "enables," or "allows." Here are some full sufficient assumption statements:

- Which of the following, if assumed, allows the conclusion to be drawn properly?
- The conclusion follows the premise logically if which of the following is assumed?
- The conclusion is properly inferred if which of the following is assumed?

Telling apart necessary assumption from sufficient assumption is kind of difficult. In a nutshell, here is what each of them is asking:

- Sufficient assumption questions ask you to find an assumption that guarantees the validity of the conclusion; it's like finding the missing piece of a puzzle.

- Necessary assumption questions ask you to find an assumption in the argument that has to be true in order for the argument's logical reasoning to have a chance at being true.

Let's look at an example of a sufficient assumption question:

If the adjuster can't make it out to Jacqueline's property by September 15 or an alternate adjuster cannot be found, her family will not be able to go on their cruise to the Bahamas. An alternative adjuster is out of the question because Jacqueline's insurance will only cover this one specific adjuster. Therefore, Jacqueline and her family will not be able to go to the Bahamas.

The conclusion follows the premise logically if which of the following is assumed?

a. Jacqueline should switch insurance companies; a good insurance company will always provide an alternate adjuster.
b. The adjuster is not available to visit before September 15 because of the chaos relating to the most recent disaster in Hurricane Andy.
c. The adjuster will be available on September 7th through 9th, and they are able to go to Jacqueline's property and look around.
d. In recent years, the Bahamas has become a tourist trap and is no longer seen as the paradise it once was.
e. Jacqueline and her family are lucky to have insurance on their home, as most people will experience natural disasters without insurance to help them afterward.
This question was created by APEX Test Prep and is not an official LSAC question.

Choice *B* is the correct answer. The argument says if the adjuster can't make it out by September 15 *or* an alternate adjuster can't be found, then the family cannot go to the Bahamas. We see that an alternate adjuster cannot be found. Ok, great. But what about the other condition? Can an adjuster make it out by

September 15? The passage does not tell us, so we must look for this information in the answers. Choice *B* validates the conclusion because it tells us that no, an adjuster cannot get to Jacqueline's house by the 15th. Let's look at the argument in abstract terms:

If Not X and Not Y, then Z. Not Y, Therefore Z.

We are looking for this:

If Not X and Not Y, then Z. Not X and Not Y, Therefore, Z.

In the abstract statement above, the "Not X" is the statement that must be assumed in order for the conclusion to be true. Let's look at the rest of the answer choices:

Choice *A* is incorrect; this tells us what Jacqueline should do in the future and does not give any indication of validating the conclusion—that Jacqueline and her family will not make it to the Bahamas. Choice *C* is incorrect; if this assumption were true, our conclusion would be invalid. We are looking for assumptions that *validate* our conclusion. If the adjuster is able to come, then Jacqueline's family *would* be able to go to the Bahamas, and the conclusion is that they *are not able* to go to the Bahamas. Choice *D* is incorrect; this is information outside of the argument and has no relevance to the conclusion. Choice *E* is incorrect; whether or not we assume this information to be true, that Jacqueline is "lucky" to have insurance, the conclusion is not validated because of it. Mark this choice as incorrect.

Identifying and Applying Principles or Rules
Principle questions on the LSAT logical reasoning portion of the exam are similar to other question types in that they deal with parallel reasoning questions, strengthening questions, and weakening questions, among others. Principle questions, however, use more general concepts to set up questions rather than specific situations. A principle is a fundamental truth that serves for a basis of reasoning or a belief system. Basically, principles offer a direction to what one should or should not do in a given situation. On the LSAT, it's important to remember that the world of the question is always true, regardless of whether it is true in real life. Therefore, principle questions on the LSAT must be accepted as true, no matter what logic or "real life" tells us.

Principle questions will have different scenarios in the question stem. The questions asked may be one of the following:

- Which one of the general principles most supports the argument above?
- The situation described above most closely conforms to which of the following principles?
- The argument above most closely conforms to which of the following generalizations?
- Which one of the following principles, if valid, most helps to justify the decision above?

Here is an example of a principle question:

In the 1990's, DEA agent Sandra O'Neal's primary purpose was to catch the largest cocaine traffickers coming in and out of Colombia. The problem with this scenario was that O'Neal had to work with an alternate cartel in order to catch the biggest and most dangerous cartel: Medellín. DEA agent Herald Luego fought O'Neal with this decision and tried everything he could to stop her from "getting in bed with the devil." To O'Neal, her actions were justified when they caught the leader of the Medellín cartel. However, Luego still disagrees with the tactics to this day.

Agent Herald Luego's ideas about drug enforcement pertaining to Sandra O'Neal most closely conforms to which of the following principles?

a. The good of the majority is always the best outcome.
b. If a person repents of a crime, he or she deserves mercy.
c. Do unto others as you would have them do unto you.
d. A favorable outcome does not excuse crimes committed to achieve it.
e. Above all, one must respect personal privacy.
This question was created by APEX Test Prep and is not an official LSAC question.

We see that the moral principle that Agent Herald Luego most likely conforms to is answer choice *D:* a favorable outcome does not excuse crimes committed to achieve it. Luego does not agree with O'Neal's actions to catch the main cartel because her means to catch this cartel are morally corrupt, and thus do not justify the end result. Luego's principles would assert that everything to catch the main cartel is done by the book, no matter what, because of what his principles state. For principle questions, if one upholds a certain principle, they must make up their mind to enforce that principle in whatever situation. Choice *A* would most likely align with Agent O'Neal's principles: the good of the majority is always the best outcome, so this is incorrect. Choices *B*, *C*, and *E* do not apply to this particular situation.

Less Common Question Types

Passage Completion
Passage completion questions leave part of the argument blank and ask you to choose the answer that logically completes it. Test takers need to take the argument's logic, structure, and tone into account when answering. As such, it's critical that you identify extreme language. For example, if the argument is nuanced and you're asked to complete the conclusion, the correct answer will not be a broad generalization.

Let's look at an example of a passage completion question:

Historian: Prior to the American Revolution, the Founding Fathers didn't want to pay new taxes, which were minimal and justifiable. Great Britain was only trying to collect money it spent protecting the American colony during the French and Indian War. The Founding Fathers also resented Britain's prohibition on westward expansion. Given the early American government's decision to legalize slavery disenfranchised ninety-five percent of the population, the Founding Fathers clearly weren't motivated by a commitment to liberty or democracy. As such, the Founding Fathers primarily initiated the American Revolution to _____.

Which of the following statements best completes the last sentence according to the author's argument?

a. expand westward
b. legalize slavery
c. guarantee liberty and spread democracy
d. avoid paying any taxes
e. revoke the new taxes and secure more land
This question was created by APEX Test Prep and is not an official LSAC question.

The blank completes the historian's conclusion, and Choice *E* is the correct answer. The argument includes two premises—anger over taxes and westward expansion. Choice *A* is wrong because it's incomplete, as the Founding Fathers also wanted to avoid paying the new taxes. Although the American government did legalize slavery, it's unclear whether slavery was illegal in the American colonies based on the argument. Plus, this answer doesn't reference the other premises. Thus, Choice *B* is incorrect. Choice *C* is incorrect because it's directly contradicted by the argument. Choice *D* doesn't reflect the other major premise, and the argument doesn't say the Founding Fathers wanted to avoid paying *any* taxes, just new taxes.

Must-Be-True
Must-be-true questions are a stronger version of inference questions. Instead of asking for a statement that's likely true based on the argument, these questions are asking what absolutely must be true. Extreme language plays an outsized role in must-be-true questions because it's easier to prove something might be true than that it must be true. So, extreme language should be checked carefully, particularly when dealing with absolutes.

Let's look at an example of a must-be-true question:

Customers are more likely to buy products when they can relate to the salesperson on a personal level. Consequently, a salesperson needs to be outgoing and personable, or else they won't ever make any sales. However, they don't always need to be knowledgeable about their products, though that definitely helps. Customers are generally happier with the product when the salesperson is knowledgeable, and every happy customer will eventually become a repeat customer. Bindee is a salesperson, and she recently sold Joseph a new mattress.

Given the statement above, which of the following MUST be true?

    a. Joseph is happy with his mattress.
    b. Joseph will eventually be a repeat customer.
    c. Joseph could relate to Bindee on a personal level.
    d. Bindee is outgoing and personable.
    e. Bindee is knowledgeable about mattresses.
    This question was created by APEX Test Prep and is not an official LSAC question.

Bindee is a salesperson who sold Joseph a mattress, and according to the passage, only a salesperson who is outgoing and personable can make sales. Thus, Choice *D* is the correct answer. The other answer choices all might be true, but none of them must be true. We know customers are generally happier with the product if the salesperson is knowledgeable, but we don't know if Bindee is knowledgeable. Unlike the outgoing and personable proposition, only some salespeople are knowledgeable about their products. Thus, Choices *A* and *E* are incorrect. Because we don't definitively know whether Joseph is a happy customer, we also don't know if he will be a repeat customer, so Choice *B* is incorrect. According to the passage, customers are more likely to buy products when they can relate to the salesperson, but that's not an absolute proposition either, so Choice *C* is incorrect.

Argument-Proceeds-By
Argument-proceeds-by questions ask about the author's method of reasoning. Sometimes these questions appear as a single argument, but they could also include a conversation and ask how the parties respond to each other. Test makers will include overly complex language and structure, so sometimes it's useful to paraphrase the argument. Aside from identifying the premises and conclusions, you should pay attention to how the premises relate to each other, as well as to the conclusion.

Let's look at an example of an argument-proceeds-by question:

There is no city ordinance that outlaws smoking on public property. Tate lives in a co-op apartment building, and a recent hurricane had just demolished his balcony. The damage included a shattered glass table and lost umbrella. The co-op's board of directors passed a resolution that fines anyone who smokes within fifty feet of the front entrance. However, the board can only fine people for violating a city ordinance. The board recently fined Tate two hundred dollars for smoking on public property during the hurricane. Tate likely won't have to pay the fine if he appeals.

Which of the following statements most accurately describes how the argument proceeds?

    a. The argument describes an irrelevant city ordinance and then applies that city ordinance to a fact pattern.
    b. The argument launches into a narrative story to provide context and concludes with irrelevant information.
    c. The argument states the most critical information at the outset and then goes on a loosely related tangent.
    d. The argument states a pertinent city ordinance, presents a mix of relevant and irrelevant facts, and then ultimately offers a conclusion.
    e. The argument presents a series of events without ever establishing how they are interconnected.
    This question was created by APEX Test Prep and is not an official LSAC question.

The argument's first sentence states a pertinent city ordinance, and it's followed by a mix of relevant and irrelevant facts. The hurricane information is irrelevant, but the board's limitations are highly relevant. Combined with the city ordinance, the board's limitations are how the argument reaches its ultimate conclusion. Thus, Choice *D* is the correct answer. The city ordinance isn't irrelevant, so Choice *A* is incorrect. The argument ends with a conclusion, not irrelevant information, so Choice *B* is incorrect. The first sentence arguably presents the most critical information because the ordinance partially determines the outcome, but the rest of the argument isn't a loosely related tangent. Thus, Choice *C* is incorrect. All of the events are interconnected, so Choice *E* is also incorrect.

Syllogism
Syllogism questions contain two or more propositions and then ask for something that absolutely must be true. Syllogisms are a classic form of argumentation that date back to Aristotle, and they're traditionally simple three-line arguments: major premise, minor premise, and conclusion. Syllogisms on the Logical Reasoning section, however, can be considerably more complex. The best way to tackle a syllogism question is to break down the argument into conditional statements. Generally speaking, the correct answer will likely be an inference that cuts out a link in the chain.

Let's look at an example of a simple logic chain:

    A → B

    B → C

Therefore, A → C

Because A → B → C is true, the B conditional can be cut out, so A → C is also true.

Now let's tackle a syllogism question:

All garbage collectors wear red shirts, and every red shirt has a collar. Some garbage collectors wear jackets, but no garbage collectors wear fur coats. Shorts cannot be worn with collared shirts, but collared shirts are always worn with boots. Jasmine is a garbage collector.

If the statements above are correct, what must be true?

   a. Jasmine is not wearing boots.
   b. Jasmine is wearing a jacket.
   c. Jasmine is not wearing a jacket.
   d. Jasmine is wearing shorts.
   e. Jasmine is not wearing shorts.
   This question was created by APEX Test Prep and is not an official LSAC question.

We know Jasmine is a garbage collector, so she must be wearing a red shirt. Based on that, let's break down all of the relevant propositions into conditional statements:

Red shirt → Collared shirt

Shorts → ~~Collared shirt~~

Collared shirt → Boots

Now we can immediately rule out Choice *A*. Jasmine is wearing a collared shirt, so she must be wearing boots. Choices *B* and *C* are also incorrect because only some garbage collectors wear jackets, so neither is necessarily true. We're left with choices that involve shorts.

To bring some clarity into the situation, let's flip that conditional to get the contrapositive:

Shorts → ~~Collared shirt~~

Collared shirt → ~~Shorts~~

Thus, Choice *E* is the correct answer. Jasmine is wearing a collared shirt, so she must not be wearing shorts.

Identifying Explanations

Explanation questions are another kind of question type on the LSAT Logical Reasoning section. Note that these are interchangeable for "Paradox Questions" or "Discrepancy Questions." Explanation questions ask you to find an explanation for one thing in particular, or for something that seems paradoxical. First, it's helpful to designate what the paradox or phenomenon is in the question stem. Then, you must look for the answer that best explains or resolves the phenomenon in a logical way.

The following examples are what explanation questions look like:

   • Which one of the following, if true, most helps to explain the difference . . .?
   • Which one of the following, if true, will resolve the discrepancy above?
   • Which of the following, if true, most helps to explain the phenomenon depicted above?
   • Which one of the following, if true, most helps to resolve the above paradox?

For explanation questions, note that you will be asked to resolve a set of statements that seem to contradict each other. A paradox is a proposal that seems self-contradictory or absurd at first, but after close inspection, it actually resolves the issue or is proven to be true.

Let's look at an example of a paradox question below:

> At the turn of the twenty-first century, Portugal reformed many of its drug use policies, including decriminalization of drugs and social policy changes centered on health. In 2014, there were only fifteen drug-related deaths in Portugal compared to 112 in 2000.

Which one of the following, if true, most helps to resolve the apparent paradox?

We are looking for an answer explanation that will solve the paradox of this statement. Typically, we would expect drug use and drug-related deaths to skyrocket if people were not being punished for drug use. However, this is not the case.

The following might be a valid reason why the opposite of what we expected to happen has happened:

People in possession of drugs are now being sent to treatment facilities instead of prison; treatment facilities have higher success rates in preventing relapse and empowering addicts to stop drug use opposed to punitive measures used inside prisons.

The explanation above helps to explain the paradox of the lowering of drug-related deaths. Social policy changes as well as decriminalization have both had a hand in the reduction of deaths. Some answer choices might try to throw you off by talking about deaths in other countries, or may throw in an answer choice meant to confuse the reality of the stem. Don't fall for these. What's stated in the question stem is the end-all. You are simply looking for the most reasonable explanation that resolves the paradox within the statements.

LSAT Analytical Reasoning

The Analytical Reasoning section of the LSAT is intended to assess the deductive capabilities of the test taker by presenting a scenario that must adhere to certain conditions or rules. The test taker must then answer questions to determine if they have appropriately understood and applied those conditions. The prompts are not necessarily based on law topics. However, the skills used to solve these problems are also necessary to work through law issues based on a variety of laws and regulations. Situations like cases involving complicated contract terms or cases with contradicting facts can require similar logic and reasoning to the logic problems presented on this section of the LSAT.

The premise and parameters usually require either grouping, matching, ordering, or a combination of the three. The test taker must analyze the parameters to determine the relationship or possible relationships that exist between the persons, things, or events discussed in the premise. Each premise will have a set of questions that address it. Examples of prompts include the seating arrangements for a dinner party, the order of subjects taught at school, and matching employees to job titles and duties.

The types of problems in the Analytical Reasoning section test for the following skills:

- Understanding structure

- Analyzing if/then statements

- Inferring possibilities

- Comprehending rules of logic

Time-Saving Tips

Like the other sections, the Analytical Reasoning section tests students' time management skills as much as anything else. In fact, most test takers find it the most difficult to complete in the allotted time. As such, you should not only practice the different types of questions but also develop and hone a plan of attack. Because there are typically four games per thirty-five minutes, you should try to complete each game in around eight minutes. Most students find that it's beneficial to spend the bulk of that time diagramming because a strong diagram will allow for questions to be answered more efficiently. Remember to keep in mind that each question has an objectively true answer. So, there's less of a need to check every answer choice like there is on the Logical Reasoning and Reading Comprehension sections, which typically ask for the "best answer."

Practice is important for all three sections, but it's especially imperative for the Analytical Reasoning section. Test takers generally do the worst on the Analytical Reasoning section on their first attempt due to it being more alien than the other sections; however, test takers also generally find that this section is the easiest to improve through practice. That's because there are only five different types of games, which are all discussed below. So, if you learn these games' structures, then you will be able to increase your pace and accuracy.

Some test takers will find one type of question more approachable than the rest. If that's the case, then it might be worth trying to identify those games and attack them first. Test takers might want to consider spending their first minute identifying the type of games and placing them in order from easiest to hardest. However, once you start diagramming a game, then it's generally better to complete all the questions you can. Reading the setup and diagramming take so much time that it's best to answer all the questions you can before leaving it behind. There are two exceptions to keep in mind. First, if you don't understand the game or your initial diagram doesn't work, it's generally more efficient to skip that game and come back later. Second, if you're spending more than 10 minutes on the game, especially on one of the first couple of games, then it might be time to skip ahead. You'll still have your diagram to come back to if time allows.

It's also important to remember that all questions aren't created equal. Some questions will be more difficult than others, such as those that add a new rule. If you find yourself spending more than a couple of minutes on a question without making progress, then it's time to consider moving on. In addition, some questions will contain answer choices that are directly contradicted by the rules. Always make sure to cross those answer choices out, even for the questions you end up skipping. In the event that you need to guess, eliminating obviously incorrect answers can dramatically increase your probability of guessing correctly.

Understanding Structure

Recognizing the different structures of the puzzles used in this section can give additional insight into solving them. All the games involve placing elements in positions or relationships. In grouping type problems, the test taker will be asked to place the variables into two or three categories like putting people on teams or doing chores on certain days of the week. Sometimes the number of variables in each category are fixed, but other times, they are not. When working through a matching type problem, there are two sets of variables, but they will not be put into a particular order. Rather, the two sets of variables will be matched together like people and the types of homes they live in or restaurants and their featured dishes. Ordering, or sequencing, type games involve assigning the elements provided into set spots using a 1:1 ratio. For example, a sequencing problem may require the test taker to find the correct order for seven plays to compete in a competition with seven spots.

Analyzing If/Then Statements

If/then statements are a common type of rule presented in analytical reasoning exercises. These statements consist of two pieces of information that relate or connect to each other. If A, then B, with A and B being conditions. Therefore, if condition A occurs, then condition B must also occur. These types of statements can be further classified as fixed or variable. An example of a fixed if/then statement would be, if John buys the green shoes, then Judy will buy the red shoes. There is only one way to apply these two conditions. The following is an example of a variable statement: If John buys the green shoes, then Judy will buy either the red shoes or the blue shoes. The second condition is not fixed. Another type of condition sometimes found in these puzzles is an either/or statement, which suggests two alternative scenarios. Either the school will get the grant, or the library will get the grant.

Inferring Possibilities

Understanding the rules presented in the logic puzzles and deciphering how they come together will help determine the possible outcomes of the situations given. Inferences are arrived at after examining the evidence (in this case, the information from the prompt and the conditions) and applying reasoning. Generally, inferences are made based on which statements are most supported by the system of information given. Sometimes, rules clearly state parts of the solution, but other times, the test taker must consider the deeper implications of each condition. It is not necessary to ascertain the complete sequence or match up of test items as there are often multiple correct combinations.

Comprehending Rules of Logic

Completing the Analytical Reasoning section of the LSAT requires a solid foundation in logic rules and theories. Test takers must be familiar with different logical indicator words and conditional statements. If/then statements were previously discussed, but test takers should also be able to recognize contrapositives, compound statements, and logically equivalent statements. Contrapositives occur when the conditions in an if/then statement take on the opposite meaning. Contrapositives have the form if not B, then not A. If/then statements can be converted to contrapositives to glean additional information. Compound statements contain two or more logic operations. For example, if Ron is stressed or tired, he will bite his nails. This compound statement provides two truths. One, if Ron is stressed, he will bite his nails. Two, if Ron is tired, he will bite his nails. Other logically equivalent statements can be derived by substituting information with the same meaning into different rules and conditions to arrive at additional solutions.

Reading the Passage Carefully

A careful reading of the prompt and the conditions is the first step to comprehending the necessary information to solve these problems and identifying the type of structure being used. The type of structure will help determine where and how the other information will fit together. Once the type of problem is identified, the conditions and questions can be read. When reading the conditions, it is important to interpret the rules correctly. Test takers must be careful not to read additional information into the conditions that is not warranted. The conditions are not meant to be tricky; they are intended to be taken at face value. Finding additional implications based on logical reasoning is part of the process, but not assuming other truths based on where something is presented in the condition or outside information not specifically mentioned in the text.

Question Independence

The next step is to read the question. The question may give additional rules that apply only to that question. This may require drawing a question-specific diagram or making a notation to reinforce that rule. The answer choices must be examined to see which do not conform to the given rules and regulations. This can often be done by using the original diagram created or by making additional inferences based on that particular question. It is also important to treat and answer each question independently. Only the original rules and prompt should be applied to every question that relates to that prompt. Test takers must be mindful of question wording, as the language is usually very specific and determining what the question is asking for will be key to arriving at the correct answer.

Rules

Loose versus Tight Rules
Rules can generally be classified as loose or tight. A *loose rule* allows for multiple interpretations, while a *tight rule* says something very specific. Generally speaking, tight rules are more valuable because they provide more concrete information, which means it's easier to make deductions. Compare the following two rules:

Alicia finished the race after Harry.

Jackson finished the race immediately before Larry.

The first rule is loose because it only tells us that Harry finished before Alicia. Harry could have finished just before Alicia, or one or more people could be between them. In contrast, the second rule is tight because it creates a definitive relationship between Jackson and Larry. If we can deduce where one of them finished, we'll know exactly where the other finished as well. This is why tight rules create more actionable deductions. Any additional information about Jackson or Larry will impact both of them because they're now interconnected.

Double Negatives

Test makers will sometimes phrase rules in double negatives. A *double negative* means that the negatives cancel each other out, meaning the sentence can be read in the affirmative. So, if you see the word *not* or any other variation of a negative, make sure you read carefully. It's well worth taking an extra second to correctly translate a rule because a mistake can lead to incorrect deductions, throwing off your entire diagram. Consider the following rule:

Horace is not one of the runners who failed to finish the race before Ron.

"Failed" is functioning as a negative in this sentence, so what this rule actually means is that Horace finished the race before Ron. Although rare, rules can also be written in the triple negative. While double negatives cancel each other out, a triple negative means the sentence is still read in the negative.

Rule Busters

Rule busters are rules that allow you to immediately rule out answer choices. This is important because the more answer choices you can eliminate, then the higher your chances of guessing correctly if time forces your hand. Consider the rule from our previous example:

Jackson finished the race immediately before Larry.

Consequently, any answer choice that has any other participant placed immediately before Larry can be ruled out. In addition, any answer choice that has anyone other than Larry immediately after Jackson can be ruled out. In general, strict rules with concrete information are more useful rule busters than conditional or abstract loose rules. Rule busting is another reason why it's useful to make as many deductions as possible before moving on to the questions. The stronger your deductions, then the more rule busters you'll have at your disposal. Some test takers find it useful to highlight rule busters to emphasize their importance.

Diagramming and Symbols

The most important part of diagramming is to be accurate and concise. Symbols should be used to create abbreviated representations for the people or things in the games. Most test takers use the first letter of the word as the symbol. Test makers don't usually use names that begin with the same letter, but if they do, make sure to differentiate between symbols by using the first two or three letters.

When drawing your diagram, make sure you have enough space by using scrap paper, blank pages, or a large chunk of open space under the question.

Examples of diagrams include:

Basic Diagram for Assignment, Ordering and Selection Games:

___ ___ ___ ___ ___ ___

Basic Diagram for Connecting Games:

	A	B	C	D
F				
G				
H				

Information should also be added to the diagram where appropriate to increase its practicality, and word banks can be used to house all of the symbols. Once your diagram is drawn, it's time to plot the rules on the diagram. In general, strict rules with concrete information are easier to plot on a diagram. For example, if we have a rule that says Charles finished third in the race, our diagram would look like this:

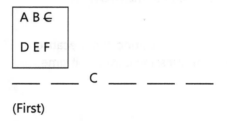

(First)

Other rules can be represented by showing where the characters can't be placed. For example, if another rule says David didn't finish before or after Charles, our diagram would look like this:

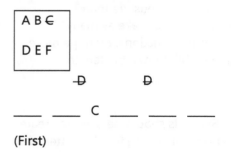

(First)

If we know two people or things are directly next to each other but don't know where they should go, we can leave a note near the diagram. For example, if we know Eileen and Felix finished the race in that order, we would write EF above the diagram.

Highlighting Text and Using Diagrams

Highlighting or noting important information can help with synthesizing and remembering crucial details. Many test takers find it helpful to create a diagram that represents the description of the scenario with places for conclusions and assumptions to be entered in. This can give the test taker a clear visual picture of the information presented and where deduction is necessary to fill in the blanks. Effectively visualizing the relationships inherent in the rules of the game will assist in answering questions quickly and clearly.

The Five Common Structures

Selection

Selection games will provide rules for selecting a smaller group of people or things out of a larger group. Typically, the setup will provide a list of people or things, and the rules will describe which of the members can or cannot be grouped together. Oftentimes there will be different specialties for each position in the group. The questions will then ask you to select different groups, and you can deduce information based on who is included and excluded. Common examples of assignment games include selecting members of a work group or selecting items for a restaurant's dinner menu.

Let's look at an example of a selection game:

A manager is creating three-person work groups out of his employees—Benjamin, Dylan, Carl, Jackie, Kyle, Lawrence, Xavier, Yolanda, and Zachary. Benjamin, Dylan, and Lawrence are accountants. Carl, Jackie, and Xavier are salespeople. Kyle, Yolanda, and Zachary are technicians. A group is formed according to the following conditions:

Each group must have one accountant, one salesperson, and one technician.

- No member can be in multiple groups.

- Dylan must be in Zachary's group.

- Benjamin and Jackie can't be in the same group.

- If Benjamin is in the group, then Carl can't be in that same group.

We know this is a selection game because there's a list of people, and we're asked to create smaller groups out of that list. To make things easier, we can also denote each person's position with an exponent in a word bank as follows:

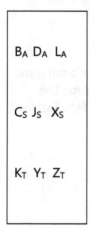

$$B_A \quad D_A \quad L_A$$

$$C_S \quad J_S \quad X_S$$

$$K_T \quad Y_T \quad Z_T$$

Because the first rule tells us there are three members per group, we can draw three blank spaces labeled with an abbreviation for each position.

— — —

A   S   T

We should now translate the other rules. $D_A \rightarrow Z_T$ ($\cancel{Z_T} \rightarrow \cancel{D_A}$) represents Dylan needing to be in Zachary's group. $B_A \rightarrow \cancel{J_S}$ ($J_S \rightarrow \cancel{B_A}$) represents Benjamin and Jackie not being in the same group. $B_A \rightarrow \cancel{C_S}$ ($C_S \rightarrow \cancel{B_A}$) represents Benjamin and Carl not being in the same group.

Because Benjamin cannot be in either Carl or Jackie's group, we can make the deduction that if Benjamin is in the group, so is Xavier, which can be represented as $B_A \rightarrow X_S$ ($\cancel{X_S} \rightarrow \cancel{B_A}$).

Now let's look at an example question:

Which one of the following is a valid group?

    a. Benjamin, Dylan, and Yolanda
    b. Benjamin, Carl, and Yolanda
    c. Benjamin, Jackie, and Kyle
    d. Benjamin, Xavier, and Kyle
    e. Kyle, Xavier, and Zachary
    This question was created by APEX Test Prep and is not an official LSAC question.

We can immediately eliminate Choices *A* and *E* because they both include two people with the same specialty. Likewise, we can eliminate Choices *B* and *C* because Benjamin can't be in either Carl or Jackie's groups. This leaves us with Choice *D* as the correct answer, which also fits our deduction that if Benjamin is in the group, then Xavier must also be in that group.

Aside from asking for a possible group, selection game questions will also provide a new rule and ask who would be on the group under that hypothetical. The same method would be used for those questions, except that it would incorporate the new rule.

Assignment
Assignment games are the same as selection games except the list is sorted into multiple subgroups. Like selection games, the setup will provide a list of people or things; rules will describe which of the members can or cannot be grouped together; and questions will then ask you about the smaller groups.

Let's look at an example of an assignment game:

A restaurant is creating its weekend menu for Friday, Saturday, and Sunday. Each day will have a different entrée for breakfast, lunch, and dinner. The breakfast entrées are muffins, pancakes, and omelets. The lunch entrées are salads, quesadillas, and tacos. The dinner entrées are angus, casserole, and fish. Each day's entrees are decided based on the following rules:

    1. Muffins are always served on the same day as quesadillas.

    2. Omelets are only served on Friday.

    3. Salads are only served on Sunday.

    4. Quesadillas are always served on the same day as angus.

Our initial diagram would look like this:

```
B: M, P, O̶



L: S̶, Q, T



D: A, C, F
```

```
F:  O  __ __
    B  L  D

Sa: __ __ __
    B  L  D

Su: __ S  __
    B  L  D
```

Our first and fourth rules create a deduction that completes an entire day's meal. If muffins are served, then quesadillas are served the same day, and if quesadillas are served, then angus is served the same day (M → Q → A). So, one of the days must serve muffins, quesadillas, and angus. In addition, because omelets are only served on Friday, and salads are only served on Sunday, muffins, quesadillas, and angus must be the entrees for Saturday.

Furthermore, because omelets are only served on Friday and muffins must be served on Saturday, then pancakes must be served on Sunday. Similarly, because salads are only served on Sunday and quesadillas must be served on Saturday, then tacos must be served on Friday.

As a result, we can nearly complete the diagram:

```
B: M̶, P̶, O̶



L: S̶, Q̶, T̶



D: A̶, C, F
```

45

```
F:   O    T    __
     B    L    D

Sa:  M    Q    A
     B    L    D

Su:  P    S    __
     B    L    D
```

Now, let's look at a couple of questions:

Which of the following must be an entrée served on Sunday?

    a. Casserole
    b. Fish
    c. Pancakes
    d. Omelets
    e. Tacos
    This question was created by APEX Test Prep and is not an official LSAC question.

We immediately know Choice *D* is incorrect because omelets are only served on Friday. Likewise, Choice *E* cannot be correct because tacos must be served Friday. Choices *A* and *B* could be correct, but they don't need to be. Either could be served on Sunday, so they are both incorrect. Thus, Choice *C* is the correct answer, which matches our diagram.

If fish is served on Sunday, then what must be served on Friday?

    a. Angus
    b. Casserole
    c. Muffins
    d. Pancakes
    e. Quesadillas
    This question was created by APEX Test Prep and is not an official LSAC question.

We can immediately rule out Choices *A*, *C*, and *E* because we know they all must be served Saturday. Similarly, Choice *D* is incorrect because pancakes can only be served on Sunday. Thus, Choice *B* is the correct answer. This also matches our diagram because if we place fish on Sunday, that leaves casserole for Friday.

Ordering
Ordering games will provide a list of people or things and then rules for placing them in a definite chronological order. When the setup mentions a schedule or sequence, then it's probably an ordering game. Test takers generally find ordering games to be the most approachable because they are straightforward. Rather than grouping or connecting different items, ordering games only focus on linear order. Common examples of ordering games include books on a shelf, seating arrangements, lines of people, races, and programming schedules.

Let's look at an example of an ordering game:

Eight high school students are seated in the front row of the auditorium at a school play. Those students are Alfred, Bruce, Christopher, Delilah, Erica, Frederick, Georgia, and Henrietta. From left to right, the seats are numbered from 1 to 8, and the order of the students must obey the following conditions:

- Christopher must be seated next to Henrietta.

- Alfred must not be seated after Georgia.

- Georgia must be seated after Bruce.

- Delilah cannot be seated next to Frederick.

- Erica must be seated in the sixth seat.

Our rules give us one important piece of concrete information—Erica must be seated in the sixth seat. We can translate the rest of the rules to:

C/H, H/C

A → G

B → G

~~D/F, F/D~~

E₆

We can combine the second and third rule to create a rule that says A and B → G. In addition, we can make a deduction that because Georgia must be seated after Alfred and Bruce, then Georgia cannot be in either the first or second seat.

So, our preliminary diagram looks like this:

A, B, C, D,

~~E~~, F, G, H

~~G~~   ~~G~~

__ __ __ __ __ E __ __
1   2   3   4   5   6   7   8

We don't have a lot of information to work with, but this isn't uncommon for ordering games. The questions will provide more information, and we can use trial and error to rule out answer choices that violate rules.

Let's look at a sample question:

Which one of the following could be the correct order of students from the fifth to eighth seat?

> a. Alfred, Erica, Georgia, Bruce
> b. Alfred, Erica, Bruce, Frederick
> c. Bruce, Georgia, Delilah, Frederick
> d. Bruce, Henrietta, Christopher, Georgia
> e. Christopher, Erica, Alfred, Georgia
> *This question was created by APEX Test Prep and is not an official LSAC question.*

We can immediately rule out Choices *C* and *D* because they don't have Erica in the sixth seat. Choice *A* is incorrect because Bruce must be seated before Georgia. Similarly, Choice *B* is incorrect because if Alfred and Bruce are seated in the fifth and seventh seat, respectively, then Frederick cannot be in the eighth seat; Georgia must be in that seat. Thus, Choice *E* is correct, and we know that to be true because it doesn't violate any rules. Accordingly, Henrietta would be in the fourth seat, and Frederick and Delilah would be in the first and third seats, leaving Bruce in the second seat, which would position him before Georgia.

Connecting

Connecting games have a setup with two lists of people or things and then provide rules for matching those people or things to each other. Sometimes the items from one list will be grouped together and then connected with the other list; however, other times the items from one list are simply matched to the other list individually. Common examples of connecting games include matching people to meals, employees to tasks, or students to activities.

Let's look at an example of a connecting game.

Ryan, Tonya, Wallace, and Zed all work at a high school tutoring program. The tutoring program offers services in English, History, Math, and Science. The workers tutor subjects according to the following rules:

- Ryan and Tonya tutor all of the same subjects.

- Wallace and Zed do not tutor any of the same subjects.

- Tonya tutors history.

- Wallace tutors math.

- Zed tutors English but not history.

- If Ryan tutors English, then Zed tutors science.

Because Wallace tutors math, then Zed must not tutor math. In addition, since Zed tutors English, then Wallace must not tutor English.

Our diagram so far looks as follows:

	E	M	S	H
R				✓
T				✓
W	X	✓		
Z	✓	X		X

$$T = R$$

$$W \neq Z$$

$$R_E \rightarrow Z_S$$

$$(\cancel{Z_S} \rightarrow \cancel{R_E})$$

Now, let's look at a couple of sample questions:

If Zed does not tutor science, which of the following must be true?

    a. Ryan tutors science.
    b. Ryan tutors English.
    c. Tonya does not tutor English.
    d. Wallace tutors science.
    e. Wallace does not tutor science.
    This question was created by APEX Test Prep and is not an official LSAC question.

If Zed does not tutor science, then based on the contrapositive of the sixth rule ($\cancel{Z_S} \rightarrow \cancel{R_E}$), Ryan does not tutor English. Because Ryan and Tonya tutor the same subjects, then Tonya also does not tutor English. Thus, Choice *C* is the correct answer. Choices *A*, *D*, and *E* all could be true, but we don't know whether any of them must be true, so they're incorrect. Choice *B* is incorrect because it violates the contrapositive of the sixth rule.

If Ryan tutors English but not math, which of the following must be true?

    a. Tonya does not tutor English.
    b. Tonya tutors math.
    c. Wallace tutors science.
    d. Wallace does not tutor science.
    e. Zed does not tutor science.
    This question was created by APEX Test Prep and is not an official LSAC question.

If Ryan tutors English, then Zed tutors science, and Zed and Wallace do not tutor any of the same subjects; therefore, Choice *D* is correct because Wallace does not tutor science. Choice *A* is incorrect because if Ryan tutors English, then Tonya tutors English. Likewise, Choice *B* is incorrect because if Ryan does not tutor math, then Tonya does not tutor math. Choices *C* and *E* are both incorrect because if Ryan tutors English, then Zed must tutor science and Wallace cannot tutor the same subject as Zed.

Hybrid

As the name implies, *hybrid* games will combine two types of games to create something unique, so there's no hard-and-fast rule on how to approach them. Some might even be unique to that year's LSAT. However, a strong understanding of the other game types will make hybrid games as approachable as any other. Let's dive into an example of a hybrid game:

Brett is the coach of a baseball team. He needs to pick the last five players in his lineup and decide on what order they will bat. The players under consideration are Abigail, Bobby, Cassandra, Dennis, Edward, Freddy, Gil, and Holly. The lineup and batting order will be chosen based on the following rules:

- Cassandra and Freddy will either play together or not at all.

- If Holly plays, then Dennis will not play.

- If they both play, Bobby will bat before Dennis.

- If they both play, Bobby will bat before Edward.

- If Gil plays, then he bats first.

- If Cassandra does not play, then Dennis plays.

We know this is a combination of selection and ordering games because it includes more players than can fit in the group and mentions placing the selected players in order. Our initial diagram looks like this:

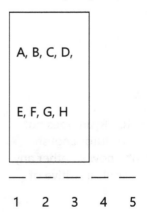

$$\underline{\quad} \ \ \underline{\quad} \ \ \underline{\quad} \ \ \underline{\quad} \ \ \underline{\quad}$$

1   2   3   4   5

We can also translate the rules into the following:

C → F (F̶ →C̶)

H → D̶ (D → H̶)

BD

BE

G_1

C̶ → D (D̶ → C)

50

We can further make the following two deductions. First, if Holly plays then Cassandra and Freddy play (H → D̶ → C → F). Second, if Dennis doesn't play then Cassandra and Freddy play (D̶ → C → F).

Now, let's look at an example question:

Which of the following could be the players Brett picks in the correct batting order from first to last?

    a. Cassandra, Freddy, Holly, Edward, Bobby
    b. Cassandra, Freddy, Holly, Edward, Gil
    c. Cassandra, Bobby, Dennis, Edward, Abigail
    d. Gil, Abigail, Cassandra, Freddy, Holly
    e. Bobby, Gil, Dennis, Edward, Abigail
    This question was created by APEX Test Prep and is not an official LSAC question.

We immediately know Choices *B* and *E* are incorrect because if Gil plays, then he bats first. Choice *A* is incorrect because if both Edward and Bobby play, Bobby bats before Edward. Choice *C* is incorrect because if Cassandra plays, then Freddy must also play. Thus, Choice *D* is the correct answer.

Sample Questions

The following are some examples of the types of prompts, conditions, and questions that are included on the Analytical Reasoning section of the test.

Passage 1
Six students are practicing a musical solo at today's rehearsal. To accommodate the students' schedule and the instrument availability, the following rules must be followed:

- The drum solo must be rehearsed after the tuba solo.
- The flute and the guitar are practiced one directly after the other.
- The piano cannot be played in the first or second rehearsal spot.
- The violin is practiced second.

1. Which of the following could be the order of the rehearsal?
    a. violin, drum, flute, guitar, tuba, piano
    b. tuba, violin, flute, guitar, drum, piano
    c. piano, violin, tuba, guitar, flute, drum
    d. tuba, flute, violin, guitar, piano, drum
    e. violin, piano, tuba, guitar, flute, drum
    This question was created by APEX Test Prep and is not an official LSAC question.

1. B: The order of tuba, violin, flute, guitar, drum, and piano could be the order of the rehearsal because it does not break any of the rules provided. Choice A could not be correct because the violin must be practiced in the second spot. Also, the drum solo must be rehearsed after the tuba solo, not before. Choice C is not the correct order because the piano cannot be rehearsed in the first or second rehearsal spot. Choice D is not correct because the flute and the guitar should be practiced directly after one another. Also, this choice does not have the violin listed in the second spot as it needs to be. Choice E is not the correct order because the violin is not practiced second, and the piano is played in the second spot. Both of these are violations of the listed conditions.

2. If the flute must be played after the drum, which of the following could be true?
    a. The flute could be played in the fourth spot.
    b. The flute could be played in the third spot.
    c. The flute could be played before the violin.
    d. The flute could be played before the tuba.
    e. The flute could be played between the drum and the piano.
    This question was created by APEX Test Prep and is not an official LSAC question.

2. A: If the flute must be played after the drum, then the flute could be played in the fourth spot. A possible rehearsal schedule that incorporates this new rule with the original rules is tuba, violin, drum, flute, guitar, and piano. Choice B would be impossible because the tuba comes before the drum, and the violin must be in the second spot. So, the earliest the flute could be played is in the fourth spot. Choice C could not be true because the violin must be played in the second spot, and as stated previously, the earliest the flute could be played is the fourth spot. Choice D is incorrect because the flute could not be played before the tuba. The flute must be played after the drum, and according to the original rules, the drum must be played after the tuba. Choice E is incorrect because the flute and the guitar must be played directly after one another to follow the original rules.

Passage 2
A group of coworkers—Hal, Seth, Claire, Joan, Ethan, and Zoe—attend a meeting. They all sit at a round table in the conference room. Their seating arrangement adheres to the following conditions:

- Joan must sit between Claire and Ethan.
- Seth cannot sit beside Ethan.
- If Zoe sits next to Claire, then she does not sit next to Hal.

1. Which of the following is a possible seating arrangement for the meeting?
    a. Joan, Hal, Ethan, Seth, Zoe, Claire
    b. Claire, Joan, Ethan, Seth, Hal, Zoe
    c. Ethan, Joan, Claire, Hal, Zoe, Seth
    d. Hal, Seth, Zoe, Claire, Joan, Ethan
    e. Ethan, Claire, Seth, Zoe, Hal, Joan
    This question was created by APEX Test Prep and is not an official LSAC question.

1. D: A possible seating arrangement that meets all the conditions in the passage is Hal, Seth, Zoe, Claire, Joan, Ethan. In this arrangement, Joan is between Claire and Ethan, which adheres to the first rule. Seth is not next to Ethan, which abides by the second rule. Zoe is next to Claire, but not Hal, which means that the third rule is also satisfied. Choice A is not a possible seating arrangement because Joan is not between Claire and Ethan, and Seth is sitting next to Ethan. Choice B is does not meet the conditions because Seth is next to Ethan, and Zoe is seated next to Hal and Claire. Choice C is not correct because Seth and Ethan are next to each other due to the round table configuration. Choice E is not a possible seating arrangement because Joan is not sitting between Claire and Ethan.

2. If Ethan is between Joan and Zoe, which of the following could be true?
    a. Claire is sitting next to Zoe.
    b. Seth cannot sit next to Hal.
    c. Claire is sitting between Joan and Seth.
    d. Claire is sitting between Seth and Hal.
    e. Joan is sitting next to Seth.
    This question was created by APEX Test Prep and is not an official LSAC question.

2. C: The statement that could be true is that Claire is sitting between Joan and Seth. This does not violate the conditions in the prompt and aligns with the additional information that Ethan is sitting between Joan and Zoe. Choice A is not correct because Claire must be sitting next to Joan who is sitting on one side of Ethan with Zoe on the other. Choice B is not supported by any of the conditions. Choice D is not true because Claire must be next to Joan so she cannot have Hal and Seth on each side of her. Choice E is incorrect because Joan must sit between Claire and Ethan.

Passage 3

Four men visit a local flower shop to buy flowers for Valentine's Day. Sam, Dave, Jeff, and Kyle must choose from roses, lilies, daisies, or tulips. They must then choose a vase for their flowers from a selection of red, pink, clear, and silver vases. Each man picks one type of flower and one vase with no overlapping choices.

Their purchases are consistent with the following:

- Sam does not choose roses or a clear vase.
- Jeff purchases daisies.
- If Dave picks a silver vase, then Kyle must pick the red vase.
- Kyle did not choose tulips.
- The man who purchases roses chooses the silver vase.

1. If Dave purchases a silver vase, what color vase and flowers does Sam choose?
   a. Pink, tulips
   b. Red, tulips
   c. Clear, lilies
   d. Pink, roses
   e. Red, daisies
   This question was created by APEX Test Prep and is not an official LSAC question.

1. A: A table or diagram can be used to determine what vase and flowers Sam chose. The conditions can be used to fill in the information in the table. 1. If Dave purchased the silver vase, he also purchased the roses. 2. If Dave picked the silver vase, then Kyle must have picked the red vase. 3. Sam did not choose the clear vase, so the only other color vase left that he could pick is the pink. 4. Because there is only the clear vase left, that means Jeff chose the clear vase. 5. Jeff purchased the daisies. 6. Kyle did not choose tulips, so the only flower left he could have chosen is the lilies. 7. The only type of flower still remaining is the tulips, so Sam must have purchased the tulips. The table below shows the information recorded for each step in the problem-solving process.

Man	Vase	Flower
Sam	3. Pink	7. Tulips
Dave	1. Silver	1. Roses
Jeff	4. Clear	5. Daisies
Kyle	2. Red	6. Lilies

2. Which of the following could be true?
   a. Jeff purchases the silver vase.
   b. Sam chooses daisies.
   c. Kyle purchases the red vase and the tulips.
   d. Sam picks the silver vase.
   e. Dave chooses the clear vase and the tulips.
   This question was created by APEX Test Prep and is not an official LSAC question.

2. E: The only choice that can be true is that Dave chooses the clear vase and the tulips. Choice A is incorrect because if Jeff purchased the silver vase, he would have also purchased roses, not daisies. Choice B is not true because Jeff chose the daisies, so Sam cannot. Choice C is incorrect because the conditions state Kyle did not choose tulips. Choice D cannot be true because if Sam purchases the silver vase, he would have to purchase roses, but the conditions state that he did not.

Reading Comprehension

Topic, Main Idea, and Supporting Details

The *topic* of a text is the general subject matter. Text topics can usually be expressed in one word, or a few words at most. Additionally, readers should ask themselves what point the author is trying to make. This point is the *main idea* or *primary purpose* of the text, the principal thing the author wants readers to know concerning the topic. Once the author has established the main idea, he or she will support the main idea by supporting details. Supporting details are evidence that support the main idea and include personal testimonies, examples, or statistics.

One analogy for these components and their relationships is that a text is like a well-designed house. The topic is the roof, covering all rooms. The main idea is the frame. The supporting details are the various rooms. To identify the topic of a text, readers can ask themselves what or who the author is writing about in the paragraph. To locate the main idea, readers can ask themselves what one idea the author wants readers to know about the topic. To identify supporting details, readers can put the main idea into question form and ask, "what does the author use to prove or explain their main idea?"

Let's look at an example. An author is writing an essay about the Amazon rainforest and trying to convince the audience that more funding should go into protecting the area from deforestation. The author makes the argument stronger by including evidence of the benefits of the rainforest: it provides habitats to a variety of species, it provides much of the earth's oxygen which in turn cleans the atmosphere, and it is the home to medicinal plants that may be the answer to some of the world's deadliest diseases. Here is an outline of the essay looking at topic, main idea, and supporting details:

- Topic: Amazon rainforest
- Main Idea: The Amazon rainforest should receive more funding to protect it from deforestation.
- Supporting Details:
    - 1. It provides habitats to a variety of species.
    - 2. It provides much of the earth's oxygen, which, in turn, cleans the atmosphere.
    - 3. It is home to medicinal plants that may treat some of the world's deadliest diseases.

Notice that the topic of the essay is listed in a few key words: "Amazon rainforest." The main idea tells us what about the topic is important: that the topic should be funded in order to prevent deforestation. Finally, the supporting details are what author relies on to convince the audience to act or to believe in the truth of the main idea.

Information that is Explicitly Stated

In the Reading Comprehension section of the LSAT, test takers will be asked questions based on their direct knowledge of the passage. The information explicitly stated in the passage leaves the reader no room for confusion. The sections below allow test takers to determine what type of information is explicitly stated in the passage. Readers should consider the following questions when reviewing a passage: Is the information an author's opinion or an objective fact? Does the information contain bias or stereotype? And within the information stated, what words are directly stated and what words leave room for a connotative interpretation?

Being cautious of the author's presentation of information will aid the test taker in determining the correct answer choice for the question stem.

Facts and Opinions

A fact is a statement that is true empirically or an event that has actually occurred in reality, and can be proven or supported by evidence; it is generally objective. In contrast, an opinion is subjective, representing something that someone believes rather than something that exists in the absolute. People's individual understandings, feelings, and perspectives contribute to variations in opinion. Although facts are typically objective in nature, in some instances, a statement of fact may be both factual and yet also subjective. For example, emotions are individual subjective experiences. If an individual says that they feel happy or sad, the feeling is subjective, but the statement is factual; hence, it is a subjective fact. In contrast, if one person tells another that the other is feeling happy or sad—whether this is true or not— that is an assumption or an opinion.

Biases

Biases usually occur when someone allows their personal preferences or ideologies to interfere with what should be an objective decision. In personal situations, someone is biased towards someone if they favor them in an unfair way. In academic writing, being biased in your sources means leaving out objective information that would turn the argument one way or the other. The evidence of bias in academic writing makes the text less credible, so be sure to present all viewpoints when writing, not just your own, so to avoid coming off as biased. Being objective when presenting information or dealing with people usually allows the author to gain more credibility.

Stereotypes

Stereotypes are preconceived notions that place a particular rule or characteristics on an entire group of people. Stereotypes are usually offensive to the group they refer to or to allies of that group, and often have negative connotations. The reinforcement of stereotypes isn't always obvious. Sometimes stereotypes can be very subtle and are still widely used in order for people to understand categories within the world. For example, saying that women are more intuitive or nurturing than men is a stereotype, although this is still an assumption used by many in order to understand differences between one another.

Denotation and Connotation

Denotation refers to a word's explicit definition, like that found in the dictionary. Denotation is often set in comparison to connotation. Connotation is the emotional, cultural, social, or personal implication associated with a word. Denotation is more of an objective definition, whereas connotation can be more subjective, although many connotative meanings of words are similar for certain cultures. The denotative meanings of words are usually based on facts, and the connotative meanings of words are usually based on emotion.

Here are some examples of words and their denotative and connotative meanings in Western culture:

Word	Denotative Meaning	Connotative Meaning
Home	A permanent place where one lives, usually as a member of a family.	A place of warmth; a place of familiarity; comforting; a place of safety and security. "Home" usually has a positive connotation.
Snake	A long reptile with no limbs and strong jaws that moves along the ground; some snakes have a poisonous bite.	An evil omen; a slithery creature (human or nonhuman) that is deceitful or unwelcome. "Snake" usually has a negative connotation.
Winter	A season of the year that is the coldest, usually from December to February in the northern hemisphere and from June to August in the southern hemisphere.	Circle of life, especially that of death and dying; cold or icy; dark and gloomy; hibernation, sleep, or rest. Winter can have a negative connotation, although many who have access to heat may enjoy the snowy season from their homes.

Information or Ideas that can be Inferred

One technique authors often use to make their fictional stories more interesting is not giving away too much information by providing hints and descriptions. It is then up to the reader to draw a conclusion about the author's meaning by connecting textual clues with the reader's own pre-existing experiences and knowledge. Drawing conclusions is important as a reading strategy for understanding what is occurring in a text. Rather than directly stating who, what, where, when, or why, authors often describe story elements. Then, readers must draw conclusions to understand significant story components. As they go through a text, readers can think about the setting, characters, plot, problem, and solution; whether the author provided any clues for consideration; and combine any story clues with their existing knowledge and experiences to draw conclusions about what occurs in the text.

Making Predictions

Before and during reading, readers can apply the strategy of making predictions about what they think may happen next. For example, what plot and character developments will occur in fiction? What points will the author discuss in nonfiction? Making predictions about portions of text they have not yet read prepares readers mentally, and also gives them a purpose for reading. To inform and make predictions about text, the reader can do the following:

- Consider the title of the text and what it implies
- Look at the cover of the book
- Look at any illustrations or diagrams for additional visual information
- Analyze the structure of the text
- Apply outside experience and knowledge to the text

Readers may adjust their predictions as they read. Reader predictions may or may not come true in text.

Making Inferences

Authors describe settings, characters, characters' emotions, and events. Readers must infer to understand the text fully. Inferring enables readers to figure out meanings of unfamiliar words, make predictions about upcoming text, draw conclusions, and reflect on reading. Readers can infer about text before, during, and after reading. In everyday life, we use sensory information to infer. Readers can do the same with text. When authors do not answer all reader questions, readers must infer by looking at illustrations, considering characters' behaviors, and asking questions during reading. Taking clues from text and connecting text to prior knowledge help to draw conclusions. Readers can infer word meanings, settings, reasons for occurrences, character emotions, pronoun referents, author messages, and answers to questions unstated in text.

Making inferences and drawing conclusions involve skills that are quite similar: both require readers to fill in information the author has omitted. Authors may omit information as a technique for inducing readers to discover the outcomes themselves; or they may consider certain information unimportant; or they may assume their reading audience already knows certain information. To make an inference or draw a conclusion about text, readers should observe all facts and arguments the author has presented and consider what they already know from their own personal experiences. Readers can determine correct and incorrect choices based on the information in the passage. For example, from a text passage describing an individual's signs of anxiety while unloading groceries and nervously clutching their wallet at a grocery store checkout, readers can infer or conclude that the individual may not have enough money to pay for everything.

The Purpose of Words or Phrases as Used in Context

Readers can often figure out what unfamiliar words mean without interrupting their reading to look them up in dictionaries by examining context. Context includes the other words or sentences in a passage. One common context clue is the root word and any affixes (prefixes/suffixes). Another common context clue is a synonym or definition included in the sentence. Sometimes both exist in the same sentence. Here's an example:

> Scientists who study birds are *ornithologists*.

Many readers may not know the word *ornithologist*. However, the example contains a definition (scientists who study birds). The reader may also have the ability to analyze the suffix (*-logy*, meaning the study of) and root (*ornitho-*, meaning bird).

Another common context clue is a sentence that shows differences. Here's an example:

> Birds *incubate* their eggs outside of their bodies, unlike mammals.

Some readers may be unfamiliar with the word *incubate*. However, since we know that "unlike mammals," birds incubate their eggs outside of their bodies, we can infer that *incubate* has something to do with keeping eggs warm outside the body until they are hatched.

In addition to analyzing the etymology of a word's root and affixes and extrapolating word meaning from sentences that contrast an unknown word with an antonym, readers can also determine word meanings from sentence context clues based on logic. Here's an example:

> Birds are always looking out for *predators* that could attack their young.

The reader who is unfamiliar with the word *predator* could determine from the context of the sentence that predators usually prey upon baby birds and possibly other young animals. Readers might also use the context clue of etymology here, as *predator* and *prey* have the same root.

When readers encounter an unfamiliar word in text, they can use the surrounding context—the overall subject matter, specific chapter/section topic, and especially the immediate sentence context. Among others, one category of context clues is grammar. For example, the position of a word in a sentence and its relationship to the other words can help the reader establish whether the unfamiliar word is a verb, a noun, an adjective, an adverb, etc. This narrows down the possible meanings of the word to one part of speech. However, this may be insufficient. In a sentence that many birds *migrate* twice yearly, the reader can determine the word is a verb, and that it probably does not mean eat or drink. It could, however, mean travel, mate, lay eggs, hatch, or molt.

Some words can have a number of different meanings depending on how they are used. For example, the word *fly* has a different meaning in each of the following sentences:

- "His trousers have a fly on them."
- "He swatted the fly on his trousers."
- "Those are some fly trousers."
- "They went fly fishing."
- "She hates to fly."
- "If humans were meant to fly, they would have wings."

As strategies, readers can try substituting a familiar word for an unfamiliar one and see whether it makes sense in the sentence. They can also identify other words in a sentence, offering clues to an unfamiliar word's meaning.

The Organization or Structure

Text structure is the way in which the author organizes and presents textual information so readers can follow and comprehend it. One kind of text structure is sequence. This means the author arranges the text in a logical order from beginning to middle to end. There are three types of sequences:

- Chronological: ordering events in time from earliest to latest

- Spatial: describing objects, people, or spaces according to their relationships to one another in space

- Order of Importance: addressing topics, characters, or ideas according to how important they are, from either least important to most important or most important to least importance

Chronological sequence is the most common sequential text structure. Readers can identify sequential structure by looking for words that signal it, like *first, earlier, meanwhile, next, then, later, finally,* or the inclusion of specific times and dates the author includes as chronological references.

Problem-Solution Text Structure
The problem-solution text structure organizes textual information by presenting readers with a problem and then developing its solution throughout the course of the text. The author may present a variety of alternatives as possible solutions, eliminating each as they are found unsuccessful, or gradually leading up to the ultimate solution. For example, in fiction, an author might write a murder mystery novel and have the character(s) solve it through investigating various clues or character alibis until the killer is identified.

In nonfiction, an author writing an essay or book on a real-world problem might discuss various alternatives and explain their disadvantages or why they would not work before identifying the best solution. For scientific research, an author reporting and discussing scientific experiment results would explain why various alternatives failed or succeeded.

Comparison-Contrast Text Structure

Comparison identifies similarities between two or more things. *Contrast* identifies differences between two or more things. Authors typically employ both to illustrate relationships between things by highlighting their commonalities and deviations. For example, a writer might compare Windows and Linux as operating systems, and contrast Linux as free and open-source vs. Windows as proprietary. When writing an essay, sometimes it is useful to create an image of the two objects or events you are comparing or contrasting. Venn diagrams are useful because they show the differences as well as the similarities between two things. Once you've seen the similarities and differences on paper, it might be helpful to create an outline of the essay with both comparison and contrast. Every outline will look different because every two or more things will have a different number of comparisons and contrasts. Say you are trying to compare and contrast carrots with sweet potatoes. Here is an example of a compare/contrast outline using those topics:

- Introduction: State why you are comparing and contrasting the foods. Give the thesis statement.
- Body paragraph 1: Sweet potatoes and carrots are both root vegetables (similarity)
- Body paragraph 2: Sweet potatoes and carrots are both orange (similarity)
- Body paragraph 3: Sweet potatoes and carrots have different nutritional profiles (difference)
- Conclusion: Restate the purpose and key points of your comparison/contrast essay.

Of course, if there is only one similarity between your topics and two differences, you will want to rearrange your outline. Always tailor your essay to what works best with your topic.

Descriptive Text Structure

Description can be both a type of text structure and a type of text. Some texts are descriptive throughout entire books. For example, a book may describe the geography of a certain country, state, or region, or tell readers all about dolphins by describing their various characteristics. Many other texts are not descriptive throughout, but use descriptive passages within the overall text. The following are a few examples of descriptive texts:

- When the author describes a character in a novel
- When the author sets the scene for an event by describing the setting.
- When a biographer describes the personality and behaviors of a real-life individual
- When a historian describes the details of a particular battle within a book about a specific war
- When a travel writer describes the climate, people, foods, and/or customs of a certain place

A hallmark of description is using sensory details, painting a vivid picture so readers can imagine it almost as if they were experiencing it personally.

Cause and Effect Text Structure

When using cause and effect to extrapolate meaning from text, readers must determine the cause when the author only communicates effects. For example, if a description of a child eating an ice cream cone includes details like beads of sweat forming on the child's face and the ice cream dripping down her hand faster than she can lick it off, the reader can infer or conclude it must be hot outside. A useful technique for making such decisions is wording them in "If/then" form, like the following: "If the child is perspiring and the ice cream melting, it must be a hot day." Cause and effect text structures explain why certain events or actions resulted in particular outcomes. For example, to explain how the dodo was hunted into extinction, an author might describe America's historical large flocks of dodo birds, the fact that gunshots did not startle/frighten dodos, and that because dodos did not flee, settlers killed whole flocks in one hunting session.

The Application of Information in the Selection to a New Context

There will be questions on the LSAT that give a scenario with a general conclusion and ask you to apply that general conclusion to a new context. Skills for making inferences and drawing conclusions will be helpful in the first portion of this question. Reading the initial scenario carefully and finding the general concept, or the bigger picture, is necessary for when the test taker attempts to apply this general concept to the new context the question provides. Here is an example of a test question that asks the test taker to apply information in a selection to a new context:

The placebo effect is a phenomenon used in clinical trial studies to test the effectiveness of new medications. A group of people are given either the new medication or the placebo but are not told which they receive. Interestingly, about one-third of people who are given the placebo in clinical trials will report a cessation of their symptoms. In one trial in 1925, a group of people were given sugar pills and told their migraines should dissipate as a result of the pills. Forty-two percent noticed that in the following six months, their weekly migraines evaporated. Researchers believe that human belief and expectation might be a reason that the placebo will work in some patients.

Considering the phenomenon of the placebo effect, what would probably happen to someone who is given a shot with no medication and told their arm should go numb from it?

    a. The patient might experience some burning in their arm, but then they would feel nothing.
    b. The patient would feel their arm going numb, as the placebo effect is certain to work.
    c. Nothing would happen because the shot does not actually have any medication in it.
    d. The individual might actually experience a numbing sensation in their arm, as the placebo works on some people by simply being told the placebo will have certain effects.
    e. The patient's arm will hurt more than normal because the placebo effect will increase their discomfort.
    This question was created by APEX Test Prep and is not an official LSAC question.

The answer is Choice *D*. The individual might actually experience a numbing sensation in their arm, as the placebo works on some people by simply being told the placebo will have certain effects. Choices *B* and *C* are too absolute to be considered correct—watch out for words like "never" or "always" in the answer choices so you can rule them out if possible. Choice *A* is incorrect because we don't know what the initial sensation of the shot would feel like for this individual. The placebo effect would have a chance of working with the shot, just like it would have a chance of working in the above example with the pill. The patient's belief in an effect is what can possibly manifest the desired result of the placebo. Choice *E* is incorrect. Although there's no medication in the injection so the arm may hurt, this would be the opposite of the placebo effect.

Principles that Function in the Selection

In the LSAT Reading Comprehension section, there will be several questions that ask the test taker about principles expressed in the selection. A principle functions as a fundamental truth used as a basis for a scenario or system of reasoning. Principles are able to function in three ways: (1) principles as the cause of something or as a final cause; (2) principles as moral, juridical, or scientific law; and (3) principles as axiom or self-evident truths.

Principles as Cause

Principles can function in different ways according to the way we express the principle. For the circumstance of cause and effect, principle refers to the cause that was efficient for the effect to come into existence. The principle as cause is traced back to Aristotelian reasoning, which surmises that every event is moved by something prior to it, or has a cause.

Principles as Law

We see principles as law at work in moral law, juridical law, and scientific law. In moral law, principles are what our predecessors teach us as children. "Do unto others," or the "golden rule," is a principle that society has embedded in us so that we are able to function as a civilized people. Principles as moral law are restrictive to the individual as a way of protecting the other person, the whole, or society.

Principles in juridical law are created by the State and also function to limit the liberty of individuals in order to protect the masses. The principles formed in juridical law are written rules that seek to establish a foundation which people can adhere to. The "homestead principle" is an example of a principle in juridical law. The "homestead principle" would function as someone gaining ownership of land because they have made it into a farm, or utilized some resource that has been unused on the land prior to their cultivation of it.

Principles as scientific law function as natural laws, including the Laws of Thermodynamics or natural selection. Principles in scientific law function as laws used to predict certain phenomena that happen in nature. In this context, principles are able to predict results of future experiments. They are developed from facts and also have the ability to be strongly supported by observational evidence.

Principles as Axioms

The LSAT may also ask questions based on principles as axioms, which are statements that are given to be true or serve as a premise for something. It is important to remember that the world of the question is absolute. That is, the foundation of the passage should be unquestioned by the test taker—the principles in the passage are considered absolutely true, no matter if they seem strange. The following list includes tips and sample questions that may be asked in the principle questions:

- What is the principle expressed in the passage?
- How does the stated principle impact the passage?
- The reasoning in the passage most conforms to which of the following principles?
- Which one of the following principles, if valid, most helps to justify the reasoning in the passage?

Some questions may include two passages, where one states the principle and the other applies it. The following is an example of the type of logical thinking you will need for principle questions on the LSAT:

A mountain climbing crew is headed up Mount Everest. The leader of the crew is a man in his sixties. His son is on the crew, with ten other individuals whom he has just met. They are all tied together with a rope. A powerful avalanche occurs, and the leader's son is knocked off a portion of the cliff and is pulling the rest of the crew down with him. It is apparent to the entire crew that if they remain tied to the son, they will all die. The leader is the only man with a knife available. He takes the knife out, tells his son he loves him, and cuts the rope.

The leader's reasoning in the passage most conforms to which of the following principles?

    a. The principle that an action is just if it benefits the majority.
    b. The principle that an action is just if it benefits those you love.
    c. The principle that certain actions are ethically right if they maximize one's own interest.
    d. The principle that a consequence should be equal to the action in question.
    e. The principle that blood is thicker than water.
    This question was created by APEX Test Prep and is not an official LSAC question.

For principle questions, take each answer choice and make it absolutely true in the world of the passage. Let's look at Choice *B*. In the world of the passage, if the leader held this principle to be true, what would he have done? He probably would have done anything to save his son, even if it meant risking his own life and the life of the crew. This choice is incorrect. The same reasoning applies to Choice *E* because the saying that "blood is thicker than water" means that family ties are more important and stronger than all others. Choice *C* is also incorrect, although this might be a difficult moral question to answer. Was the leader acting in his own interest? His own life was saved in the process of letting his son go, so it can be argued this was the case. However, the flipside to this dilemma is that for the rest of his life, the leader would have to live with the death of his son, and so his best interest may have been to risk the crew's life to save his son. This would, in the long run, serve to alleviate his feelings of guilt. This principle is not the best principle to apply to the passage. Choice *D* is incorrect. This principle would apply to the leader *after the incident* when he must own up to the consequences of his actions, but it does not apply to the current situation in the passage.

Choice *A* is the correct answer choice. We see that the leader chooses to act in the best interest of the majority. He lets his son go so that the rest of the crew (the majority) does not fall off the cliff. Ultimately, this is the principle of utilitarianism, which states that an action is right if it benefits the majority. In the world of the passage, the leader is in accordance with this principle based on his actions.

Here's another example of picking out a principle that applies to the selection:

Julie is staying with her grandmother for Thanksgiving. Julie and her grandmother have disagreed many times during the vacation because Julie politely declines to eat the meals her grandmother cooks if they have meat in them. Julie also does not like participating in the cattle roping her family does for fun on the weekends. Julie's grandmother wants Julie to be part of the culture and fit in with everyone else, so Julie takes up knitting so that she can relate to her grandmother in a way that speaks to her culture.

Julie's reasoning in the passage most conforms to which of the following principles?

    a. Respect your elders and learn by their wisdom.
    b. Everything happens for a reason.
    c. Never harm, or participate in the harming of, a living thing.
    d. All animals have souls and should be treated as humans.
    e. A stitch in time can save nine.
    This question was created by APEX Test Prep and is not an official LSAC question.

Choice *A* is incorrect. The choice states to respect your elders and learn by their wisdom. Julie does attempt to respect her grandmother by learning how to knit. However, Julie would in fact sacrifice her principle (do no harm) if she were to abide by the wisdom of her elders. Julie is not trying to conform to this principle with her reasoning. Choice *B* is also incorrect. We don't see an argument about purpose or a reason for cause happening, so we can mark this one off. Choice *D* is also incorrect—all animals have souls and should be treated as humans. This one is tricky because we see Julie abstaining from participating in eating meat and from joining in certain activities with them. This one is tempting, but Choice *C* is a much clearer, broader principle we can apply to Julie's line of thinking. Choice *E* is also incorrect. Although the tie-in to knitting may be tempting, the idiom "a stitch in time saves nine" means that taking the time to right a problem immediately will save much more time and work in the long run.

Choice *C* states to never harm, or participate in the harming of, a living thing. We can tell that Julie's line of thinking conforms best with this principle. Once accepted, principles will direct a person to live one way or another. Julie has accepted not only to not harm a living thing, but to not participate in the harming of a living thing. We can see this by her refusal to eat what her grandmother prepares as well as her refusal to participate in the cattle roping. We also see Julie attempting to repair the hurt feelings between her and her grandmother.

Analogies to Claims or Arguments in the Selection

In its most basic form, an analogy compares two different things. For the LSAT, an analogy question is a situation that parallels the principles or foundations given in another situation. The source, or analogue, will require you to pick out the most apt target in a set of particular events. Analogy questions are different from principle questions in that they work with two particular situations, instead of working with applying a general principle to a particular situation. In law school, students may find that many cases are determined by precedent case law, where an analogy will be drawn based on facts from a prior case to determine the outcome of a current case.

Analogy questions in the LSAT look like the following:

Based on the hypothetical situation given in paragraph 4, which of the following is most closely analogous?

The answer choices will consist of five particular situations that attempt to mirror the hypothetical situation given in the passage. In order to find the correct answer, it might be helpful to know the basics of what an analogy is.

The following is a list of different types of analogies:

Category	Example
Part to whole	"All screwdrivers are considered tools." Tools is the whole, and screwdrivers is the part to that whole. Be careful of reversing this logic, though. It would be an error to say "Likewise, all tools are considered screwdrivers." In simplified terms, saying "All A are B" is not the same as saying "All B are A."
Confusing causation with correlation	"The number of traffic accidents in Florida has gone up this past summer. The temperature has also increased this summer by 10 degrees. I bet the heat is making drivers more irritable." This logic confuses causation (the heat is causing accidents) with correlation. Traffic accidents have gone up and so has the heat, but that doesn't necessarily mean that one is causing the other. A new smartphone could have been released, creating distracted drivers. Or, there could have been more rain in the summer, causing dangerous driving conditions.
Performer to related action	"A lawyer passes the bar exam after finishing law school." "A student passes the SAT after finishing high school." Performer to related action requires a test taker to make an association between actions and their performers. Here, we see a performer passing some kind of exam after they've gone through years of training. In this way, the student and their actions are analogous to the lawyer and their actions.
Cause and effect	"A restaurant was shut down because it had an infestation problem." "A company went out of business because it couldn't produce enough inventory." In the analogy above, we see something shutting down because of a problem. The cause and effect analogy presents an unequivocal effect to an action and requires no effort to make something happen.
Unintended consequence	"Two parents enter therapy with the purpose of finding help for their son, who is struggling with substance abuse and behavioral problems at school. As a result, they find that they also are dealing with unresolved issues in the past and learn ways to cope with these issues." Here, a group of people set out to do one thing, and receive another in return. In this situation, there is an unintended consequence beside an intended consequence. In some situations, the intended consequence might not happen at all, and the unintended consequence will have the opposite effect of the intended consequence, creating an ironic situation.

Let's look at an example of an analogy question on the LSAT Reading Comprehension section. It is a passage from *Ten Great Events in History* by James Johonnot:

Meantime, in the Church of England a spirit of criticism had grown up. Stricter thinkers disliked the imposing ceremonies which the English church still retained: some of the ministers ceased to wear gowns in preaching, performed the marriage ceremony without using a ring, and were in favor of simplifying all the church service. Unpretentious workers began to tire of the everlasting quarreling, and to long for a religion simple and quiet. These soon met trouble, for the rulers had decided that salvation was by the Church of England, as the sovereign, its head, should order. Dissent was the two-fold guilt of heresy and revolution—sin against God and crime against the king and English law. They were forbidden to preach at all if they would not wear a gown during service, and the people who went to hear them were punished. This treatment caused serious thought among the "non-conformists," as they were called, and, once thinking, they soon concluded that the king had no such supreme right to order the church, and the church had over its ministers no such right of absolute dictation.

Given Johonnot's account of the criticism of the Church of England in the Middle Ages, which one of the following is most analogous to the situation of the ministers' refusal to wear gowns and the workers' resistance of fighting leading to problems with the church?
    a. A church body meets resistance from an outside secular entity for issues related to social injustice.
    b. Three members of a sorority refuse to do the hazing ritual, so they are kicked out of the sorority by the other members.
    c. A group of kids at school who create an exclusive club that says anyone can join as long as they are in second grade and live on Magnolia Street.
    d. A book club that finds it is no longer useful to its members, and thus attempts to change the group to a film club instead.
    e. An elephant who is sick and cannot make the journey with its tribe finds it is being held up by the rest of the members of the group so that it can walk the rest of the way.
    This question was created by APEX Test Prep and is not an official LSAC question.

What we have in the original source are members part of a group refusing to participate in a tradition, so as a result, they are punished by the group. The ministers and workers are refusing to participate in church traditions, so they are punished or banished by the church.

Choice *B* is the correct answer to this analogy question. We have members of a group refusing to participate in a tradition (a hazing ritual), so they are punished by the other members of the group. This target most closely fits the original analogy.

Choice *A* is incorrect. Although we are dealing with a church, the structure of the analogy is not the same. In this situation, the group is experiencing external problems rather than internal problems depicted in the original source.

Choice *C* is incorrect because this analogy depicts a creation of a group and the rules for joining. In the original analogy, the group is already established with its laws and traditions.

Choice *D* is incorrect because this group is able to adapt to dissent as a whole, and is not in disagreement about traditions that are no longer working.

Finally, Choice *E* is incorrect. The group in question is supporting and helping a member who is sick. In the original source, the members aren't sick, but in disagreement, and they certainly aren't being supported.

An Author's Attitude as Revealed in the Tone of a Passage or the Language Used

Some question stems in the LSAT Reading Comprehension section will ask about the author's attitude toward a certain person or idea. While it may seem impossible to know exactly what the author felt toward their subject, there are clues to indicate the emotion, or lack thereof, of the author. Clues like word choice or style will alert readers to the author's attitude. Some possible words that name the author's attitude are listed below:

- Admiring
- Angry
- Critical
- Defensive
- Enthusiastic
- Humorous
- Moralizing
- Neutral
- Objective
- Patriotic
- Persuasive
- Playful
- Sentimental
- Serious
- Supportive
- Sympathetic
- Unsupportive

An author's tone is the author's attitude toward their subject and is usually indicated by word choice. If an author's attitude toward their subject is one of disdain, the author will show the subject in a negative light, using deflating words or words that are negatively charged. If an author's attitude toward their subject is one of praise, the author will use agreeable words and show the subject in a positive light. If an author takes a neutral tone towards their subject, their words will be neutral as well, and they probably will show all sides of their subject, not just the negative or positive side.

Style is another indication of the author's attitude and includes aspects such as sentence structure, type of language, and formatting. Sentence structure is how a sentence is put together. Sometimes, short, choppy sentences will indicate a certain tone given the surrounding context, while longer sentences may serve to create a buffer to avoid being too harsh, or may be used to explain additional information. Style may also include formal or informal language. Using formal language to talk about a subject may indicate a level of respect. Using informal language may be used to create an atmosphere of friendliness or familiarity with a subject. Again, it depends on the surrounding context whether or not language is used in a negative or positive way. Style may also include formatting, such as determining the length of paragraphs or figuring out how to address the reader at the very beginning of the text.

The following is a passage from *The Florentine Painters of the Renaissance* by Bernhard Berenson. Following the passage is a question stem regarding the author's attitude toward their subject:

Let us look now at an even greater triumph of movement than the Nudes, Pollaiuolo's "Hercules Strangling Antæus." As you realise the suction of Hercules' grip on the earth, the swelling of his calves with the pressure that falls on them, the violent throwing back of his chest, the stifling force of his embrace; as you realise the supreme effort of Antæus, with one hand crushing down upon the head and the other tearing at the arm of Hercules, you feel as if a fountain of energy had sprung up under your feet and were playing through your veins. I cannot refrain from mentioning still another masterpiece, this time not only of movement, but of tactile values and personal beauty as well—Pollaiuolo's "David" at Berlin. The young warrior has sped his stone, cut off the giant's head, and now he strides over it, his graceful, slender figure still vibrating with the rapidity of his triumph, expectant, as if fearing the ease of it. What lightness, what buoyancy we feel as we realise the movement of this wonderful youth!

Which one of the following best captures the author's attitude toward the paintings depicted in the passage?
   a. Neutrality towards the subject in this passage.
   b. Disdain for the violence found in the paintings.
   c. Excitement for the physical beauty found within the paintings.
   d. Passion for the movement and energy of the paintings.
   e. Seriousness for the level of artistry the paintings hold.
   This question was created by APEX Test Prep and is not an official LSAC question.

Choice *D* is the best answer. We know that the author feels positively about the subject because of the word choice. Berenson uses words and phrases like "supreme," "fountain of energy," "graceful," "figure still vibrating," "lightness," "buoyancy," and "wonderful youth." Notice also the exclamation mark at the end of the paragraph. These words and style depict an author full of passion, especially for the movement and energy found within the paintings.

Choice *A* is incorrect because the author is biased towards the subject due to the energy he writes with—he calls the movement in the paintings "wonderful" and by the other word choices and phrases, readers can tell that this is not an objective analysis of these paintings. Choice *B* is incorrect because, although the author does mention the "violence" in the stance of Hercules, he does not exude disdain towards this. Choice *C* is incorrect. There is excitement in the author's tone, and some of this excitement is directed towards the paintings' physical beauty. However, this is not the *best* answer choice. Choice *D* is more accurate when stating the passion is for the movement and energy of the paintings, of which physical beauty is included. Finally, Choice *E* is incorrect. The tone is partly serious, but we see the author getting carried away with enthusiasm for the beauty of the paintings towards the middle and especially the end of the passage.

The Impact of New Information on Claims or Arguments in the Selection

Another useful skill in the LSAT Reading Comprehension section is being able to use new information from the question stem to apply to a claim in the passage. Most of the "new information" questions in the LSAT Reading Comprehension are *strengthening* or *weakening* questions, where the question will ask which of the information in the answer choices best strengthens or weakens a given claim. It's important to read the passage a few times first in order to understand the original claim's stance. Below is a list of questions that might fall under the "new information" question stems:

   • Which of the following, if true, best strengthens the author's claim?
   • Which of the following, if true, most weakens the author's claim?
   • Which of the following, if true, best supports the author's argument that says . . .?
   • Which of the following, if true, most undermines the author's claim that says . . .?

The new information question stems will contain a synonym of the word "strengthens" or "weakens," such as "bolsters," "supports," or "undermines," and will also display the statement "if true." The latter is to make sure the test taker does not question the validity of the information in a real-world context. Just like stated above, everything in the passage or in the question stem will be assumed to be true unless otherwise stated or put into question by the stem. The following is an example of a strengthening question:

For elementary-age students, the biggest sports-related injuries are concussions incurred while playing soccer. The popular assumption is that football is more prone to causing concussions, but this is not the case for this age group. I think it would greatly benefit our school if we required our soccer players to wear helmets.

Which of the following, if true, best strengthens the author's claim above?
    a. Concussions are not life-threatening, so students should not be required to wear helmets during soccer games.
    b. Major concussions can limit a student's ability to read, write, and focus on schoolwork or any other work that demands mental attention.
    c. The school board will give a monetary incentive to any school sports program that adopts helmets.
    d. Forcing soccer players to wear helmets would be humiliating if they were playing a team that wasn't required to wear helmets.
    e. We should get rid of soccer altogether since it causes elementary-age students the most concussions out of any sport.
    This question was created by APEX Test Prep and is not an official LSAC question.

Choice *C* is the best answer because it strengthens the author's claim by presenting an even stronger reason for requiring soccer players to wear helmets. If we as readers know that there is another advantage to accepting the author's claim that players should wear helmets besides preventing concussions, then the claim is strengthened.

Choice *A* is incorrect because it states that concussions are not life-threatening. This logic does not help the argument in question, that the school would benefit from requiring students to wear helmets.

Choice *B* is tricky because it builds upon a premise in the argument. However, the author's claim is not convincing us that concussions are dangerous. The author's claim is that the school would greatly benefit from requiring players to wear helmets during soccer. This choice is close, but it is not the best choice.

Choice *D* also goes against the argument in question—the argument is that requiring soccer players to wear helmets would benefit the school, and Choice *D* gives reason *not* to require soccer players to wear helmets. This choice weakens the claim.

Choice *E* goes beyond the argument. This choice doesn't strengthen the claim; it provides another claim altogether. This choice is incorrect.

In the above example of a strengthening question, we see which new information (answer choices) strengthens the claim presented in the passage. Let's take a look at a weakening question:

Last Sunday at the Lincolnville picnic, the town ate every single one of my mom's chocolate brownies. My mom makes the best dessert in Lincolnville.

Which of the following, if true, most undermines the author's claim above?
  a. My mom went to cooking school and has her own television show dedicated to dessert recipes.
  b. My mom also brought potato salad to the picnic, but no one ate it.
  c. There were 250 people at the town picnic.
  d. My mom won the town award for "tastiest treats."
  e. Chocolate brownies were the only dessert brought to the picnic.
  This question was created by APEX Test Prep and is not an official LSAC question.

This is a basic form of a weakening question. The question stem has a premise (the town ate every single one of my mom's chocolate brownies) and a conclusion (my mom makes the best dessert in Lincolnville). In strengthening and weakening questions, it's important to look for a bridge between the premise and conclusion that will either hurt or help the conclusion. Choice *E* is the best answer choice because it most undermines, or weakens, the author's conclusion that the mom makes the best dessert in Lincolnville. If the speaker's only proof that the mom makes the best dessert in Lincolnville is that the town ate all the brownies, then the fact that brownies were the *only* dessert makes us think the town ate the brownies because that was the only option, not because they were the best dessert.

Choices *A* and *D* serve to strengthen the claim, not to weaken it. Choice *B* does not weaken or strengthen the claim because the claim has to do with desserts, and this answer choice is about potato salad. Choice *C* is incorrect because we don't know how big the town is to make a judgment on whether 250 people is an adequate representation of the community.

Again, most strengthening and weakening questions will provide some sort of gap between its premise and conclusion. The new information will make that gap stronger, weaken the gap, or be irrelevant to the claim altogether. Try not to get lost in the wording of the new information; rather, plug the new information in the passage and see how the new information works—that is, does it strengthen the claim or weaken the claim?

The Official LSAT PrepTest

16

The sample test that follows consists of four sections corresponding to the four scored sections of the LSAT.

INSTRUCTIONS FOR COMPLETING THE BIOGRAPHICAL AREA ARE ON THE BACK COVER OF YOUR TEST BOOKLET.
USE ONLY A NO. 2 OR HB PENCIL TO COMPLETE THIS ANSWER SHEET. DO NOT USE INK.

USE A NO. 2 OR HB PENCIL ONLY   ● Right Mark   ⊘ ⊗ ⊙ Wrong Marks

A

1 LAST NAME / FIRST NAME / MI

2 SOCIAL SECURITY/ SOCIAL INSURANCE NO.

3 LSAC ACCOUNT NUMBER

4 CENTER NUMBER

L

5 DATE OF BIRTH

MONTH	DAY	YEAR
Jan		
Feb		
Mar		
Apr		
May		
June		
July		
Aug		
Sept		
Oct		
Nov		
Dec		

6 TEST FORM CODE

7 RACIAL/ETHNIC DESCRIPTION
Mark one or more
- 1 Amer. Indian/Alaska Native
- 2 Asian
- 3 Black/African American
- 4 Canadian Aboriginal
- 5 Caucasian/White
- 6 Hispanic/Latino
- 7 Native Hawaiian/ Other Pacific Islander
- 8 Puerto Rican
- 9 TSI/Aboriginal Australian

8 GENDER
- Male
- Female

9 DOMINANT LANGUAGE
- English
- Other

10 ENGLISH FLUENCY
- Yes
- No

11 TEST DATE
MONTH / DAY / YEAR

12 TEST FORM

13 TEST BOOK SERIAL NO.

═══ **Law School Admission Test** ═══

Mark one and only one answer to each question. Be sure to fill in completely the space for your intended answer choice. If you erase, do so completely. Make no stray marks.

SECTION 1 — questions 1–30, answer choices A B C D E

SECTION 2 — questions 1–30, answer choices A B C D E

SECTION 3 — questions 1–30, answer choices A B C D E

SECTION 4 — questions 1–30, answer choices A B C D E

SECTION 5 — questions 1–30, answer choices A B C D E

14 PLEASE PRINT INFORMATION

LAST NAME   FIRST

SSN/SIN

DATE OF BIRTH

● Ⓑ

General Directions for the LSAT Answer Sheet

The actual testing time for this portion of the test will be 2 hours 55 minutes. There are five sections, each with a time limit of 35 minutes. The supervisor will tell you when to begin and end each section. If you finish a section before time is called, you may check your work on that section only; do not turn to any other section of the test book and do not work on any other section either in the test book or on the answer sheet.

There are several different types of questions on the test, and each question type has its own directions. Be sure you understand the directions for each question type before attempting to answer any questions in that section.

Not everyone will finish all the questions in the time allowed. Do not hurry, but work steadily and as quickly as you can without sacrificing accuracy. You are advised to use your time effectively. If a question seems too difficult, go on to the next one and return to the difficult question after completing the section. MARK THE BEST ANSWER YOU CAN FOR EVERY QUESTION. NO DEDUCTIONS WILL BE MADE FOR WRONG ANSWERS. YOUR SCORE WILL BE BASED ONLY ON THE NUMBER OF QUESTIONS YOU ANSWER CORRECTLY.

ALL YOUR ANSWERS MUST BE MARKED ON THE ANSWER SHEET. Answer spaces for each question are lettered to correspond with the letters of the potential answers to each question in the test book. After you have decided which of the answers is correct, blacken the corresponding space on the answer sheet. BE SURE THAT EACH MARK IS BLACK AND COMPLETELY FILLS THE ANSWER SPACE. Give only one answer to each question. If you change an answer, be sure that all previous marks are erased completely. Since the answer sheet is machine scored, incomplete erasures may be interpreted as intended answers. ANSWERS RECORDED IN THE TEST BOOK WILL NOT BE SCORED.

There may be more question numbers on this answer sheet than there are questions in a section. Do not be concerned, but be certain that the section and number of the question you are answering matches the answer sheet section and question number. Additional answer spaces in any answer sheet section should be left blank. Begin your next section in the number one answer space for that section.

LSAC takes various steps to ensure that answer sheets are returned from test centers in a timely manner for processing. In the unlikely event that an answer sheet is not received, LSAC will permit the examinee either to retest at no additional fee or to receive a refund of his or her LSAT fee. THESE REMEDIES ARE THE ONLY REMEDIES AVAILABLE IN THE UNLIKELY EVENT THAT AN ANSWER SHEET IS NOT RECEIVED BY LSAC.

Score Cancellation

Complete this section only if you are absolutely certain you want to cancel your score. A CANCELLATION REQUEST CANNOT BE RESCINDED. IF YOU ARE AT ALL UNCERTAIN, YOU SHOULD NOT COMPLETE THIS SECTION.

To cancel your score from this administration, you **must**:

A. fill in both ovals here ..... ○ ○
        AND

B. read the following statement. Then sign your name and enter the date.
    YOUR SIGNATURE ALONE IS NOT SUFFICIENT FOR SCORE CANCELLATION. BOTH OVALS ABOVE MUST BE FILLED IN FOR SCANNING EQUIPMENT TO RECOGNIZE YOUR REQUEST FOR SCORE CANCELLATION.

I certify that I wish to cancel my test score from this administration. I understand that my request is irreversible and that my score will not be sent to me or to the law schools to which I apply.

_____
Sign your name in full

_____
Date

FOR LSAC USE ONLY   ●

HOW DID YOU PREPARE FOR THE LSAT?
(Select all that apply.)

Responses to this item are voluntary and will be used for statistical research purposes only.

○ By studying the free sample questions available on LSAC's website.
○ By taking the free sample LSAT available on LSAC's website.
○ By working through official LSAT *PrepTests, ItemWise,* and/or other LSAC test prep products.
○ By using LSAT prep books or software not published by LSAC.
○ By attending a commercial test preparation or coaching course.
○ By attending a test preparation or coaching course offered through an undergraduate institution.
○ Self study.
○ Other preparation.
○ No preparation.

CERTIFYING STATEMENT

Please write the following statement. Sign and date.

I certify that I am the examinee whose name appears on this answer sheet and that I am here to take the LSAT for the sole purpose of being considered for admission to law school. I further certify that I will neither assist nor receive assistance from any other candidate, and I agree not to copy, retain, or transmit examination questions in any form or discuss them with any other person.

_____
_____
_____
_____
_____
_____
_____
_____
_____

SIGNATURE: _____   TODAY'S DATE: ____/____/____
                                                                                MONTH DAY YEAR

SECTION I

Time—35 minutes

24 Questions

Directions: Each group of questions in this section is based on a set of conditions. In answering some of the questions, it may be useful to draw a rough diagram. Choose the response that most accurately and completely answers each question and blacken the corresponding space on your answer sheet.

Questions 1–6

Eight new students—R, S, T, V, W, X, Y, Z—are being divided among exactly three classes—class 1, class 2, and class 3. Classes 1 and 2 will gain three new students each; class 3 will gain two new students. The following restrictions apply:

R must be added to class 1.
S must be added to class 3.
Neither S nor W can be added to the same class as Y.
V cannot be added to the same class as Z.
If T is added to class 1, Z must also be added to class 1.

1. Which one of the following is an acceptable assignment of students to the three classes?

	1	2	3
(A)	R, T, Y	V, W, X	S, Z
(B)	R, T, Z	S, V, Y	W, X
(C)	R, W, X	V, Y, Z	S, T
(D)	R, X, Z	T, V, Y	S, W
(E)	R, X, Z	V, W, Y	S, T

2. Which one of the following is a complete and accurate list of classes any one of which could be the class to which V is added?

(A) class 1
(B) class 3
(C) class 1, class 3
(D) class 2, class 3
(E) class 1, class 2, class 3

3. If X is added to class 1, which one of the following is a student who must be added to class 2 ?

(A) T
(B) V
(C) W
(D) Y
(E) Z

4. If X is added to class 3, each of the following is a pair of students who can be added to class 1 EXCEPT

(A) Y and Z
(B) W and Z
(C) V and Y
(D) V and W
(E) T and Z

5. If T is added to class 3, which one of the following is a student who must be added to class 2 ?

(A) V
(B) W
(C) X
(D) Y
(E) Z

6. Which one of the following must be true?

(A) If T and X are added to class 2, V is added to class 3.
(B) If V and W are added to class 1, T is added to class 3.
(C) If V and W are added to class 1, Z is added to class 3.
(D) If V and X are added to class 1, W is added to class 3.
(E) If Y and Z are added to class 2, X is added to class 2.

GO ON TO THE NEXT PAGE.

Questions 7–12

Four lions—F, G, H, J—and two tigers—K and M—will be assigned to exactly six stalls, one animal per stall. The stalls are arranged as follows:

First Row: 1   2   3

Second Row: 4   5   6

The only stalls that face each other are stalls 1 and 4, stalls 2 and 5, and stalls 3 and 6. The following conditions apply:

The tigers' stalls cannot face each other.
A lion must be assigned to stall 1.
H must be assigned to stall 6.
J must be assigned to a stall numbered one higher than K's stall.
K cannot be assigned to the stall that faces H's stall.

7. Which one of the following must be true?

(A) F is assigned to an even-numbered stall.
(B) F is assigned to stall 1.
(C) J is assigned to stall 2 or else stall 3.
(D) J is assigned to stall 3 or else stall 4.
(E) K is assigned to stall 2 or else stall 4.

8. Which one of the following could be true?

(A) F's stall is numbered one higher than J's stall.
(B) H's stall faces M's stall.
(C) J is assigned to stall 4.
(D) K's stall faces J's stall.
(E) K's stall is in a different row than J's stall.

9. Which one of the following must be true?

(A) A tiger is assigned to stall 2.
(B) A tiger is assigned to stall 5.
(C) K's stall is in a different row from M's stall.
(D) Each tiger is assigned to an even-numbered stall.
(E) Each lion is assigned to a stall that faces a tiger's stall.

10. If K's stall is in the same row as H's stall, which one of the following must be true?

(A) F's stall is in the same row as J's stall.
(B) F is assigned to a lower-numbered stall than G.
(C) G is assigned to a lower-numbered stall than M.
(D) G's stall faces H's stall.
(E) M's stall is in the same row as G's stall.

11. If J is assigned to stall 3, which one of the following could be true?

(A) F is assigned to stall 2.
(B) F is assigned to stall 4.
(C) G is assigned to stall 1.
(D) G is assigned to stall 4.
(E) M is assigned to stall 5.

12. Which one of the following must be true?

(A) A tiger is assigned to stall 2.
(B) A tiger is assigned to stall 4.
(C) A tiger is assigned to stall 5.
(D) A lion is assigned to stall 3.
(E) A lion is assigned to stall 4.

GO ON TO THE NEXT PAGE.

Questions 13–18

On an undeveloped street, a developer will simultaneously build four houses on one side, numbered consecutively 1, 3, 5, and 7, and four houses on the opposite side, numbered consecutively 2, 4, 6, and 8. Houses 2, 4, 6, and 8 will face houses 1, 3, 5, and 7, respectively. Each house will be exactly one of three styles—ranch, split-level, or Tudor—according to the following conditions:

Adjacent houses are of different styles.
No split-level house faces another split-level house.
Every ranch house has at least one Tudor house adjacent to it.
House 3 is a ranch house.
House 6 is a split-level house.

13. Any of the following could be a Tudor house EXCEPT house

(A) 1
(B) 2
(C) 4
(D) 7
(E) 8

14. If there is one ranch house directly opposite another ranch house, which one of the following could be true?

(A) House 8 is a ranch house.
(B) House 7 is a split-level house.
(C) House 4 is a Tudor house.
(D) House 2 is a split-level house.
(E) House 1 is a ranch house.

15. If house 4 is a Tudor house, then it could be true that house

(A) 1 is a Tudor house
(B) 2 is a Tudor house
(C) 5 is a ranch house
(D) 7 is a Tudor house
(E) 8 is a ranch house

16. On the street, there could be exactly

(A) one ranch house
(B) one Tudor house
(C) two Tudor houses
(D) four ranch houses
(E) five ranch houses

17. If no house faces a house of the same style, then it must be true that house

(A) 1 is a split-level house
(B) 1 is a Tudor house
(C) 2 is a ranch house
(D) 2 is a split-level house
(E) 4 is a Tudor house

18. If the condition requiring house 6 to be a split-level house is suspended but all other original conditions remain the same, then any of the following could be an accurate list of the styles of houses 2, 4, 6, and 8, respectively, EXCEPT:

(A) ranch, split-level, ranch, Tudor
(B) split-level, ranch, Tudor, split-level
(C) split-level, Tudor, ranch, split-level
(D) Tudor, ranch, Tudor, split-level
(E) Tudor, split-level, ranch, Tudor

GO ON TO THE NEXT PAGE.

Questions 19–24

Within a tennis league each of five teams occupies one of five positions, numbered 1 through 5 in order of rank, with number 1 as the highest position. The teams are initially in the order R, J, S, M, L, with R in position 1. Teams change positions only when a lower-positioned team defeats a higher-positioned team. The rules are as follows:

Matches are played alternately in odd-position rounds and in even-position rounds.

In an odd-position round, teams in positions 3 and 5 play against teams positioned immediately above them.

In an even-position round, teams in positions 2 and 4 play against teams positioned immediately above them.

When a lower-positioned team defeats a higher-positioned team, the two teams switch positions after the round is completed.

19. Which one of the following could be the order of teams, from position 1 through position 5 respectively, after exactly one round of even-position matches if no odd-position round has yet been played?

(A) J, R, M, L, S
(B) J, R, S, L, M
(C) R, J, M, L, S
(D) R, J, M, S, L
(E) R, S, J, L, M

20. If exactly two rounds of matches have been played, beginning with an odd-position round, and if the lower-positioned teams have won every match in those two rounds, then each of the following must be true EXCEPT:

(A) L is one position higher than J.
(B) R is one position higher than L.
(C) S is one position higher than R.
(D) J is in position 4.
(E) M is in position 3.

21. Which one of the following could be true after exactly two rounds of matches have been played?

(A) J has won two matches.
(B) L has lost two matches.
(C) R has won two matches.
(D) L's only match was played against J.
(E) M played against S in two matches.

22. If after exactly three rounds of matches M is in position 4, and J and L have won all of their matches, then which one of the following can be true?

(A) J is in position 2.
(B) J is in position 3.
(C) L is in position 2.
(D) R is in position 1.
(E) S is in position 3.

23. If after exactly three rounds M has won three matches and the rankings of the other four teams relative to each other remain the same, then which one of the following must be in position 3 ?

(A) J
(B) L
(C) M
(D) R
(E) S

24. If after exactly three rounds the teams, in order from first to fifth position, are R, J, L, S, and M, then which one of the following could be the order, from first to fifth position, of the teams after the second round?

(A) J, R, M, S, L
(B) J, L, S, M, R
(C) R, J, S, L, M
(D) R, L, M, S, J
(E) R, M, L, S, J

S T O P

IF YOU FINISH BEFORE TIME IS CALLED, YOU MAY CHECK YOUR WORK ON THIS SECTION ONLY.
DO NOT WORK ON ANY OTHER SECTION IN THE TEST.

SECTION II
Time—35 minutes
24 Questions

Directions: The questions in this section are based on the reasoning contained in brief statements or passages. For some questions, more than one of the choices could conceivably answer the question. However, you are to choose the best answer; that is, the response that most accurately and completely answers the question. You should not make assumptions that are by commonsense standards implausible, superfluous, or incompatible with the passage. After you have chosen the best answer, blacken the corresponding space on your answer sheet.

1. The city's center for disease control reports that the rabies epidemic is more serious now than it was two years ago: two years ago less than 25 percent of the local raccoon population was infected, whereas today the infection has spread to more than 50 percent of the raccoon population. However, the newspaper reports that whereas two years ago 32 cases of rabid raccoons were confirmed during a 12-month period, in the past 12 months only 18 cases of rabid raccoons were confirmed.

   Which one of the following, if true, most helps to resolve the apparent discrepancy between the two reports?

   (A) The number of cases of rabies in wild animals other than raccoons has increased in the past 12 months.
   (B) A significant proportion of the raccoon population succumbed to rabies in the year before last.
   (C) The symptoms of distemper, another disease to which raccoons are susceptible, are virtually identical to those of rabies.
   (D) Since the outbreak of the epidemic, raccoons, which are normally nocturnal, have increasingly been seen during daylight hours.
   (E) The number of confirmed cases of rabid raccoons in neighboring cities has also decreased over the past year.

2. Recently, reviewers of patent applications decided against granting a patent to a university for a genetically engineered mouse developed for laboratory use in studying cancer. The reviewers argued that the mouse was a new variety of animal and that rules governing the granting of patents specifically disallow patents for new animal varieties.

   Which one of the following, if true, most weakens the patent reviewers' argument?

   (A) The restrictions the patent reviewers cited pertain only to domesticated farm animals.
   (B) The university's application for a patent for the genetically engineered mouse was the first such patent application made by the university.
   (C) The patent reviewers had reached the same decision on all previous patent requests for new animal varieties.
   (D) The patent reviewers had in the past approved patents for genetically engineered plant varieties.
   (E) The patent reviewers had previously decided against granting patents for new animal varieties that were developed through conventional breeding programs rather than through genetic engineering.

GO ON TO THE NEXT PAGE.

Questions 3–4

Although water in deep aquifers does not contain disease-causing bacteria, when public water supplies are drawn from deep aquifers, chlorine is often added to the water as a disinfectant because contamination can occur as a result of flaws in pipes or storage tanks. Of 50 municipalities that all pumped water from the same deep aquifer, 30 chlorinated their water and 20 did not. The water in all of the municipalities met the regional government's standards for cleanliness, yet the water supplied by the 20 municipalities that did not chlorinate had less bacterial contamination than the water supplied by the municipalities that added chlorine.

3. Which one of the following can properly be concluded from the information given above?

   (A) A municipality's initial decision whether or not to use chlorine is based on the amount of bacterial contamination in the water source.
   (B) Water in deep aquifers does not contain any bacteria of any kind.
   (C) Where accessible, deep aquifers are the best choice as a source for a municipal water supply.
   (D) The regional government's standards allow some bacteria in municipal water supplies.
   (E) Chlorine is the least effective disinfecting agent.

4. Which one of the following, if true, most helps explain the difference in bacterial contamination in the two groups of municipalities?

   (A) Chlorine is considered by some experts to be dangerous to human health, even in the small concentrations used in municipal water supplies.
   (B) When municipalities decide not to chlorinate their water supplies, it is usually because their citizens have voiced objections to the taste and smell of chlorine.
   (C) The municipalities that did not add chlorine to their water supplies also did not add any of the other available water disinfectants, which are more expensive than chlorine.
   (D) Other agents commonly added to public water supplies, such as fluoride and sodium hydroxide, were not used by any of the 50 municipalities.
   (E) Municipalities that do not chlorinate their water supplies are subject to stricter regulation by the regional government in regard to pipes and water tanks than are municipalities that use chlorine.

5. The population of songbirds throughout England has decreased in recent years. Many people explain this decrease as the result of an increase during the same period in the population of magpies, which eat the eggs and chicks of songbirds.

   Which one of the following, if true, argues most strongly against the explanation reported in the passage?

   (A) Official records of the population of birds in England have been kept for only the past 30 years.
   (B) The number of eggs laid yearly by a female songbird varies widely according to the songbird's species.
   (C) Although the overall population of magpies has increased, in most areas of England in which the songbird population has decreased, the number of magpies has remained stable.
   (D) The population of magpies has increased because farmers no longer shoot or trap magpies to any great extent, though farmers still consider magpies to be pests.
   (E) Although magpies eat the eggs and chicks of songbirds, magpies' diets consist of a wide variety of other foods as well.

6. The introduction of symbols for numbers is an event lost in prehistory, but the earliest known number symbols, in the form of simple grooves and scratches on bones and stones, date back 20,000 years or more. Nevertheless, since it was not until 5,500 years ago that systematic methods for writing numerals were invented, it was only then that any sort of computation became possible.

   Which one of the following is an assumption on which the argument relies?

   (A) Grooves and scratches found on bones and stones were all made by people, and none resulted from natural processes.
   (B) Some kinds of surfaces upon which numeric symbols could have been made in the period before 5,500 years ago were not used for that purpose.
   (C) Grooves and scratches inscribed on bones and stones do not date back to the time of the earliest people.
   (D) Computation of any sort required a systematic method for writing numerals.
   (E) Systematic methods for writing numerals were invented only because the need for computation arose.

GO ON TO THE NEXT PAGE.

79

7. Politician: Now that we are finally cleaning up the industrial pollution in the bay, we must start making the bay more accessible to the public for recreational purposes.

    Reporter: But if we increase public access to the bay, it will soon become polluted again.

    Politician: Not true. The public did not have access to the bay, and it got polluted. Therefore, if and when the public is given access to the bay, it will not get polluted.

    Which one of the following most closely parallels the flawed pattern of reasoning in the politician's reply to the reporter?

    (A) If there had been a full moon last night, the tide would be higher than usual today. Since the tide is no higher than usual, there must not have been a full moon last night.

    (B) The detective said that whoever stole the money would be spending it conspicuously by now. Jones is spending money conspicuously, so he must be the thief.

    (C) When prisoners convicted of especially violent crimes were kept in solitary confinement, violence in the prisons increased. Therefore, violence in the prisons will not increase if such prisoners are allowed to mix with fellow prisoners.

    (D) To get a driver's license, one must pass a written test. Smith passed the written test, so she must have gotten a driver's license.

    (E) In order to like abstract art, you have to understand it. Therefore, in order to understand abstract art, you have to like it.

8. Because learned patterns of behavior, such as the association of a green light with "go" or the expectation that switches will flip up for "on," become deeply ingrained, designers should make allowances for that fact, in order not to produce machines that are inefficient or dangerous.

    In which one of the following situations is the principle expressed most clearly violated?

    (A) Manufacturers have refused to change the standard order of letters on the typewriter keyboard even though some people who have never learned to type find this arrangement of letters bewildering.

    (B) Government regulations require that crucial instruments in airplane cockpits be placed in exactly the same array in all commercial aircraft.

    (C) Automobile manufacturers generally design for all of their automobiles a square or oblong ignition key and a round or oval luggage compartment key.

    (D) The only traffic signs that are triangular in shape are "yield" signs.

    (E) On some tape recorders the "start" button is red and the "stop" button is yellow.

9. From 1973 to 1989 total energy use in this country increased less than 10 percent. However, the use of electrical energy in this country during this same period grew by more than 50 percent, as did the gross national product—the total value of all goods and services produced in the nation.

    If the statements above are true, then which one of the following must also be true?

    (A) Most of the energy used in this country in 1989 was electrical energy.

    (B) From 1973 to 1989 there was a decline in the use of energy other than electrical energy in this country.

    (C) From 1973 to 1989 there was an increase in the proportion of energy use in this country that consisted of electrical energy use.

    (D) In 1989 electrical energy constituted a larger proportion of the energy used to produce the gross national product than did any other form of energy.

    (E) In 1973 the electrical energy that was produced constituted a smaller proportion of the gross national product than did all other forms of energy combined.

10. A fundamental illusion in robotics is the belief that improvements in robots will liberate humanity from "hazardous and demeaning work." Engineers are designing only those types of robots that can be properly maintained with the least expensive, least skilled human labor possible. Therefore, robots will not eliminate demeaning work—only substitute one type of demeaning work for another.

    The reasoning in the argument is most vulnerable to the criticism that it

    (A) ignores the consideration that in a competitive business environment some jobs might be eliminated if robots are not used in the manufacturing process

    (B) assumes what it sets out to prove, that robots create demeaning work

    (C) does not specify whether or not the engineers who design robots consider their work demeaning

    (D) attempts to support its conclusion by an appeal to the emotion of fear, which is often experienced by people faced with the prospect of losing their jobs to robots

    (E) fails to address the possibility that the amount of demeaning work eliminated by robots might be significantly greater than the amount they create

GO ON TO THE NEXT PAGE.

80

11. If the needle on an industrial sewing machine becomes badly worn, the article being sewn can be ruined. In traditional apparel factories, the people who operate the sewing machines monitor the needles and replace those that begin to wear out. Industrial sewing operations are becoming increasingly automated, however, and it would be inefficient for a factory to hire people for the sole purpose of monitoring needles. Therefore a sophisticated new acoustic device that detects wear in sewing machine needles is expected to become standard equipment in the automated apparel factories of the future.

Which one of the following is most strongly supported by the information above?

(A) In automated apparel factories, items will be ruined by faulty needles less frequently than happens in traditional apparel factories.
(B) In the automated apparel factories of the future, each employee will perform only one type of task.
(C) Traditional apparel factories do not use any automated equipment.
(D) The needles of industrial sewing machines wear out at unpredictable rates.
(E) As sewing machine needles become worn, the noise they make becomes increasingly loud.

Questions 12–13

Alexander: The chemical waste dump outside our town should be cleaned up immediately. Admittedly, it will be very costly to convert that site into woodland, but we have a pressing obligation to redress the harm we have done to local forests and wildlife.

Teresa: But our town's first priority is the health of its people. So even if putting the dump there was environmentally disastrous, we should not spend our resources on correcting it unless it presents a significant health hazard to people. If it does, then we only need to remove that hazard.

12. Teresa's statement most closely conforms to which one of the following principles?

(A) Environmental destruction should be redressed only if it is in the economic interest of the community to do so.
(B) Resources should be allocated only to satisfy goals that have the highest priority.
(C) No expense should be spared in protecting the community's health.
(D) Environmental hazards that pose slight health risks to people should be rectified if the technology is available to do so.
(E) It is the community as a whole that should evaluate the importance of eliminating various perceived threats to public health.

13. Which one of the following is the point at issue between Alexander and Teresa?

(A) whether the maintenance of a chemical waste dump inflicts significant damage on forests and wildlife
(B) whether it is extremely costly to clean up a chemical waste dump in order to replace it by a woodland
(C) whether the public should be consulted in determining the public health risk posed by a chemical waste dump
(D) whether the town has an obligation to redress damage to local forests and wildlife if that damage poses no significant health hazard to people
(E) whether destroying forests and wildlife in order to establish a chemical waste dump amounts to an environmental disaster

GO ON TO THE NEXT PAGE.

81

14. In 1980, Country A had a per capita gross domestic product (GDP) that was $5,000 higher than that of the European Economic Community. By 1990, the difference, when adjusted for inflation, had increased to $6,000. Since a rising per capita GDP indicates a rising average standard of living, the average standard of living in Country A must have risen between 1980 and 1990.

Which one of the following is an assumption on which the argument depends?

(A) Between 1980 and 1990, Country A and the European Economic Community experienced the same percentage increase in population.

(B) Between 1980 and 1990, the average standard of living in the European Economic Community fell.

(C) Some member countries of the European Economic Community had, during the 1980s, a higher average standard of living than Country A.

(D) The per capita GDP of the European Economic Community was not lower by more than $1,000 in 1990 than it had been in 1980.

(E) In 1990, no member country of the European Economic Community had a per capita GDP higher than that of Country A.

15. Municipal officials originally estimated that it would be six months before municipal road crews could complete repaving a stretch of road. The officials presumed that private contractors could not finish any sooner. However, when the job was assigned to a private contractor, it was completed in just 28 days.

Which one of the following, if true, does most to resolve the discrepancy between the time estimated for completion of the repaving job, and the actual time taken by the private contractor?

(A) Road repaving work can only be done in the summer months of June, July, and August.

(B) The labor union contract for road crews employed by both municipal agencies and private contractors stipulates that employees can work only eight hours a day, five days a week, before being paid overtime.

(C) Many road-crew workers for private contractors have previously worked for municipal road crews, and vice versa.

(D) Private contractors typically assign 25 workers to each road-repaving job site, whereas the number assigned to municipal road crews is usually 30.

(E) Municipal agencies must conduct a lengthy bidding process to procure supplies after repaving work is ordered and before they can actually start work, whereas private contractors can obtain supplies readily as needed.

16. Researchers in South Australia estimate changes in shark populations inhabiting local waters by monitoring what is termed the "catch per unit effort" (CPUE). The CPUE for any species of shark is the number of those sharks that commercial shark-fishing boats catch per hour for each kilometer of gill net set out in the water. Since 1973 the CPUE for a particular species of shark has remained fairly constant. Therefore, the population of that species in the waters around South Australia must be at approximately its 1973 level.

Which one of the following, if true, most seriously weakens the argument?

(A) The waters around South Australia are the only area in the world where that particular species of shark is found.

(B) The sharks that are the most profitable to catch are those that tend to remain in the same area of ocean year after year and not migrate far from where they were born.

(C) A significant threat to shark populations, in addition to commercial shark fishing, is "incidental mortality" that results from catching sharks in nets intended for other fish.

(D) Most of the quotas designed to protect shark populations limit the tonnage of sharks that can be taken and not the number of individual sharks.

(E) Since 1980 commercial shark-fishing boats have used sophisticated electronic equipment that enables them to locate sharks with greater accuracy.

GO ON TO THE NEXT PAGE.

Questions 17–18

Winston: The Public Transportation Authority (PTA) cannot fulfill its mandate to operate without a budget deficit unless it eliminates service during late-night periods of low ridership. Since the fares collected during these periods are less than the cost of providing the service, these cuts would reduce the deficit and should be made. Transit law prohibits unauthorized fare increases, and fare-increase authorization would take two years.

Ping: Such service cuts might cost the PTA more in lost fares than they would save in costs, for the PTA would lose those riders who leave home during the day but must return late at night. Thus the PTA would lose two fares, while realizing cost savings for only one leg of such trips.

17. The relationship of Ping's response to Winston's argument is that Ping's response

   (A) carefully redefines a term used in Winston's argument
   (B) questions Winston's proposal by raising considerations not addressed by Winston
   (C) supplies a premise that could have been used as part of the support for Winston's argument
   (D) introduces detailed statistical evidence that is more persuasive than that offered by Winston
   (E) proposes a solution to the PTA's dilemma by contradicting Winston's conclusion

18. Which one of the following, if true, most strongly supports Ping's conclusion?

   (A) Over 23 percent of the round trips made by PTA riders are either initiated or else completed during late-night periods.
   (B) Reliable survey results show that over 43 percent of the PTA's riders oppose any cut in PTA services.
   (C) The last time the PTA petitioned for a 15 percent fare increase, the petition was denied.
   (D) The PTA's budget deficit is 40 percent larger this year than it was last year.
   (E) The PTA's bus drivers recently won a new contract that guarantees them a significant cash bonus each time they work the late-night shifts.

19. The Volunteers for Literacy Program would benefit if Dolores takes Victor's place as director, since Dolores is far more skillful than Victor is at securing the kind of financial support the program needs and Dolores does not have Victor's propensity for alienating the program's most dedicated volunteers.

The pattern of reasoning in the argument above is most closely paralleled in which one of the following?

   (A) It would be more convenient for Dominique to take a bus to school than to take the subway, since the bus stops closer to her house than does the subway and, unlike the subway, the bus goes directly to the school.
   (B) Joshua's interest would be better served by taking the bus to get to his parent's house rather than by taking an airplane, since his primary concern is to travel as cheaply as possible and taking the bus is less expensive than going by airplane.
   (C) Belinda will get to the concert more quickly by subway than by taxi, since the concert takes place on a Friday evening and on Friday evenings traffic near the concert hall is exceptionally heavy.
   (D) Anita would benefit financially by taking the train to work rather than driving her car, since when she drives she has to pay parking fees and the daily fee for parking a car is higher than a round-trip train ticket.
   (E) It would be to Fred's advantage to exchange his bus tickets for train tickets, since he needs to arrive at his meeting before any of the other participants and if he goes by bus at least one of the other participants will arrive first.

GO ON TO THE NEXT PAGE.

20. Students from outside the province of Markland, who in any given academic year pay twice as much tuition each as do students from Markland, had traditionally accounted for at least two-thirds of the enrollment at Central Markland College. Over the past 10 years academic standards at the college have risen, and the proportion of students who are not Marklanders has dropped to around 40 percent.

Which one of the following can be properly inferred from the statements above?

(A) If it had not been for the high tuition paid by students from outside Markland, the college could not have improved its academic standards over the past 10 years.

(B) If academic standards had not risen over the past 10 years, students who are not Marklanders would still account for at least two-thirds of the college's enrollment.

(C) Over the past 10 years, the number of students from Markland increased and the number of students from outside Markland decreased.

(D) Over the past 10 years, academic standards at Central Markland College have risen by more than academic standards at any other college in Markland.

(E) If the college's per capita revenue from tuition has remained the same, tuition fees have increased over the past 10 years.

21. Several years ago, as a measure to reduce the population of gypsy moths, which depend on oak leaves for food, entomologists introduced into many oak forests a species of fungus that is poisonous to gypsy moth caterpillars. Since then, the population of both caterpillars and adult moths has significantly declined in those areas. Entomologists have concluded that the decline is attributable to the presence of the poisonous fungus.

Which one of the following, if true, most strongly supports the conclusion drawn by the entomologists?

(A) A strain of gypsy moth whose caterpillars are unaffected by the fungus has increased its share of the total gypsy moth population.

(B) The fungus that was introduced to control the gypsy moth population is poisonous to few insect species other than the gypsy moth.

(C) An increase in numbers of both gypsy moth caterpillars and gypsy moth adults followed a drop in the number of some of the species that prey on the moths.

(D) In the past several years, air pollution and acid rain have been responsible for a substantial decline in oak tree populations.

(E) The current decline in the gypsy moth population in forests where the fungus was introduced is no greater than a decline that occurred concurrently in other forests.

22. Director of personnel: Ms. Tours has formally requested a salary adjustment on the grounds that she was denied merit raises to which she was entitled. Since such grounds provide a possible basis for adjustments, an official response is required. Ms. Tours presents compelling evidence that her job performance has been both excellent in itself and markedly superior to that of others in her department who were awarded merit raises. Her complaint that she was treated unfairly thus appears justified. Nevertheless, her request should be denied. To raise Ms. Tours's salary because of her complaint would jeopardize the integrity of the firm's merit-based reward system by sending the message that employees can get their salaries raised if they just complain enough.

The personnel director's reasoning is most vulnerable to criticism on the grounds that it

(A) fails to consider the possibility that Ms. Tours's complaint could be handled on an unofficial basis

(B) attempts to undermine the persuasiveness of Ms. Tours's evidence by characterizing it as "mere complaining"

(C) sidesteps the issue of whether superior job performance is a suitable basis for awarding salary increases

(D) ignores the possibility that some of the people who did receive merit increases were not entitled to them

(E) overlooks the implications for the integrity of the firm's merit-based reward system of denying Ms. Tours's request

GO ON TO THE NEXT PAGE.

23. S: People who are old enough to fight for their country are old enough to vote for the people who make decisions about war and peace. This government clearly regards 17 year olds as old enough to fight, so it should acknowledge their right to vote.

T: Your argument is a good one only to the extent that fighting and voting are the same kind of activity. Fighting well requires strength, muscular coordination, and in a modern army, instant and automatic response to orders. Performed responsibly, voting, unlike fighting, is essentially a deliberative activity requiring reasoning power and knowledge of both history and human nature.

T responds to S's argument by

(A) citing evidence overlooked by S that would have supported S's conclusion

(B) calling into question S's understanding of the concept of rights

(C) showing that S has ignored the distinction between having a right to do something and having an obligation to do that thing

(D) challenging the truth of a claim on which S's conclusion is based

(E) arguing for a conclusion opposite to the one drawn by S

24. The role of the Uplandian supreme court is to protect all human rights against abuses of government power. Since the constitution of Uplandia is not explicit about all human rights, the supreme court must sometimes resort to principles outside the explicit provisions of the constitution in justifying its decisions. However, human rights will be subject to the whim of whoever holds judicial power unless the supreme court is bound to adhere to a single objective standard, namely, the constitution. Therefore, nothing but the explicit provisions of the constitution can be used to justify the court's decisions. Since these conclusions are inconsistent with each other, it cannot be true that the role of the Uplandian supreme court is to protect all human rights against abuses of government power.

The reasoning that leads to the conclusion that the first sentence in the passage is false is flawed because the argument

(A) ignores data that offer reasonable support for a general claim and focuses on a single example that argues against that claim

(B) seeks to defend a view on the grounds that the view is widely held and that decisions based on that view are often accepted as correct

(C) rejects a claim as false on the grounds that those who make that claim could profit if that claim is accepted by others

(D) makes an unwarranted assumption that what is true of each member of a group taken separately is also true of the group as a whole

(E) concludes that a particular premise is false when it is equally possible for that premise to be true and some other premise false

S T O P

IF YOU FINISH BEFORE TIME IS CALLED, YOU MAY CHECK YOUR WORK ON THIS SECTION ONLY.
DO NOT WORK ON ANY OTHER SECTION IN THE TEST.

SECTION III
Time—35 minutes
26 Questions

<u>Directions:</u> The questions in this section are based on the reasoning contained in brief statements or passages. For some questions, more than one of the choices could conceivably answer the question. However, you are to choose the <u>best</u> answer; that is, the response that most accurately and completely answers the question. You should not make assumptions that are by commonsense standards implausible, superfluous, or incompatible with the passage. After you have chosen the best answer, blacken the corresponding space on your answer sheet.

1. The painted spider spins webs that are much stickier than the webs spun by the other species of spiders that share the same habitat. Stickier webs are more efficient at trapping insects that fly into them. Spiders prey on insects by trapping them in their webs; therefore, it can be concluded that the painted spider is a more successful predator than its competitors.

   Which one of the following, if true, most seriously weakens the argument?

   (A) Not all of the species of insects living in the painted spider's habitat are flying insects.
   (B) Butterflies and moths, which can shed scales, are especially unlikely to be trapped by spider webs that are not very sticky.
   (C) Although the painted spider's venom does not kill insects quickly, it paralyzes them almost instantaneously.
   (D) Stickier webs reflect more light, and so are more visible to insects, than are less-sticky webs.
   (E) The webs spun by the painted spider are no larger than the webs spun by the other species of spiders in the same habitat.

2. Despite the best efforts of astronomers, no one has yet succeeded in exchanging messages with intelligent life on other planets or in other solar systems. In fact, no one has even managed to prove that any kind of extraterrestrial life exists. Thus, there is clearly no intelligent life anywhere but on Earth.

   The argument's reasoning is flawed because the argument

   (A) fails to consider that there might be extraterrestrial forms of intelligence that are not living beings
   (B) confuses an absence of evidence for a hypothesis with the existence of evidence against the hypothesis
   (C) interprets a disagreement over a scientific theory as a disproof of that theory
   (D) makes an inference that relies on the vagueness of the term "life"
   (E) relies on a weak analogy rather than on evidence to draw a conclusion

GO ON TO THE NEXT PAGE.

86

Questions 3–4

Bart: A mathematical problem that defied solution for hundreds of years has finally yielded to a supercomputer. The process by which the supercomputer derived the result is so complex, however, that no one can fully comprehend it. Consequently, the result is unacceptable.

Anne: In scientific research, if the results of a test can be replicated in other tests, the results are acceptable even though the way they were derived might not be fully understood. Therefore, if a mathematical result derived by a supercomputer can be reproduced by other supercomputers following the same procedure, it is acceptable.

3. Bart's argument requires which one of the following assumptions?

(A) The mathematical result in question is unacceptable because it was derived with the use of a supercomputer.
(B) For the mathematical result in question to be acceptable, there must be someone who can fully comprehend the process by which it was derived.
(C) To be acceptable, the mathematical result in question must be reproduced on another supercomputer.
(D) Making the mathematical result in question less complex would guarantee its acceptability.
(E) The supercomputer cannot derive an acceptable solution to the mathematical problem in question.

4. The exchange between Bart and Anne most strongly supports the view that they disagree as to

(A) whether a scientific result that has not been replicated can properly be accepted
(B) whether the result that a supercomputer derives for a mathematical problem must be replicated on another supercomputer before it can be accepted
(C) the criterion to be used for accepting a mathematical result derived by a supercomputer
(D) the level of complexity of the process to which Bart refers in his statements
(E) the relative complexity of mathematical problems as compared to scientific problems

5. It is commonly held among marketing experts that in a nonexpanding market a company's best strategy is to go after a bigger share of the market and that the best way to do this is to run comparative advertisements that emphasize weaknesses in the products of rivals. In the stagnant market for food oil, soybean-oil and palm-oil producers did wage a two-year battle with comparative advertisements about the deleterious effect on health of each other's products. These campaigns, however, had little effect on respective market shares; rather, they stopped many people from buying any edible oils at all.

The statements above most strongly support the conclusion that comparative advertisements

(A) increase a company's market share in all cases in which that company's products are clearly superior to the products of rivals
(B) should not be used in a market that is expanding or likely to expand
(C) should under no circumstances be used as a retaliatory measure
(D) carry the risk of causing a contraction of the market at which they are aimed
(E) yield no long-term gains unless consumers can easily verify the claims made

6. Recent unexpectedly heavy rainfalls in the metropolitan area have filled the reservoirs and streams; water rationing, therefore, will not be necessary this summer.

Which one of the following, if true, most undermines the author's prediction?

(A) Water rationing was imposed in the city in three of the last five years.
(B) A small part of the city's water supply is obtained from deep underground water systems that are not reached by rainwater.
(C) The water company's capacity to pump water to customers has not kept up with the increased demand created by population growth in the metropolitan area.
(D) The long-range weather forecast predicts lower-than-average temperatures for this summer.
(E) In most years the city receives less total precipitation in the summer than it receives in any other season.

GO ON TO THE NEXT PAGE.

87

7. John: In 80 percent of car accidents, the driver at fault was within five miles of home, so people evidently drive less safely near home than they do on long trips.

   Judy: But people do 80 percent of their driving within five miles of home.

   How is Judy's response related to John's argument?

   (A)   It shows that the evidence that John presents, by itself, is not enough to prove his claim.
   (B)   It restates the evidence that John presents in different terms.
   (C)   It gives additional evidence that is needed by John to support his conclusion.
   (D)   It calls into question John's assumption that whenever people drive more than five miles from home they are going on a long trip.
   (E)   It suggests that John's conclusion is merely a restatement of his argument's premise.

8. Reasonable people adapt themselves to the world; unreasonable people persist in trying to adapt the world to themselves. Therefore, all progress depends on unreasonable people.

   If all of the statements in the passage above are true, which one of the following statements must also be true?

   (A)   Reasonable people and unreasonable people are incompatible.
   (B)   If there are only reasonable people, there cannot be progress.
   (C)   If there are unreasonable people, there will be progress.
   (D)   Some unreasonable people are unable to bring about progress.
   (E)   Unreasonable people are more persistent than reasonable people.

9. Theater critic: The theater is in a dismal state. Audiences are sparse and revenue is down. Without the audience and the revenue, the talented and creative people who are the lifeblood of the theater are abandoning it. No wonder standards are deteriorating.

   Producer: It's not true that the theater is in decline. Don't you realize that your comments constitute a self-fulfilling prophecy? By publishing these opinions, you yourself are discouraging new audiences from emerging and new talent from joining the theater.

   Which one of the following is a questionable technique employed by the producer in responding to the critic?

   (A)   focusing on the effects of the critic's evaluation rather than on its content
   (B)   accusing the critic of relying solely on opinion unsupported by factual evidence
   (C)   challenging the motives behind the critic's remarks rather than the remarks themselves
   (D)   relying on emphasis rather than on argument
   (E)   invoking authority in order to intimidate the critic

10. Michelangelo's sixteenth-century Sistine Chapel paintings are currently being restored. A goal of the restorers is to uncover Michelangelo's original work, and so additions made to Michelangelo's paintings by later artists are being removed. However, the restorers have decided to make one exception: to leave intact additions that were painted by da Volterra.

    Which one of the following, if true, most helps to reconcile the restorers' decision with the goal stated in the passage?

    (A)   The restorers believe that da Volterra stripped away all previous layers of paint before he painted his own additions to the Sistine Chapel.
    (B)   Because da Volterra used a type of pigment that is especially sensitive to light, the additions to the Sistine Chapel that da Volterra painted have relatively muted colors.
    (C)   Da Volterra's additions were painted in a style that was similar to the style used by Michelangelo.
    (D)   Michelangelo is famous primarily for his sculptures and only secondarily for his paintings, whereas da Volterra is known exclusively for his paintings.
    (E)   Da Volterra's work is considered by certain art historians to be just as valuable as the work of some of the other artists who painted additions to Michelangelo's work.

11. A controversial program rewards prison inmates who behave particularly well in prison by giving them the chance to receive free cosmetic plastic surgery performed by medical students. The program is obviously morally questionable, both in its assumptions about what inmates might want and in its use of the prison population to train future surgeons. Putting these moral issues aside, however, the surgery clearly has a powerful rehabilitative effect, as is shown by the fact that, among recipients of the surgery, the proportion who are convicted of new crimes committed after release is only half that for the prison population as a whole.

    A flaw in the reasoning of the passage is that it

    (A)   allows moral issues to be a consideration in presenting evidence about matters of fact
    (B)   dismisses moral considerations on the grounds that only matters of fact are relevant
    (C)   labels the program as "controversial" instead of discussing the issues that give rise to controversy
    (D)   asserts that the rehabilitation of criminals is not a moral issue
    (E)   relies on evidence drawn from a sample that there is reason to believe is unrepresentative

GO ON TO THE NEXT PAGE.

12. The retina scanner, a machine that scans the web of tiny blood vessels in the retina, stores information about the pattern formed by the blood vessels. This information allows it to recognize any pattern it has previously scanned. No two eyes have identical patterns of blood vessels in the retina. A retina scanner can therefore be used successfully to determine for any person whether it has ever scanned a retina of that person before.

The reasoning in the argument depends upon assuming that

(A) diseases of the human eye do not alter the pattern of blood vessels in the retina in ways that would make the pattern unrecognizable to the retina scanner

(B) no person has a different pattern of blood vessels in the retina of the left eye than in the retina of the right eye

(C) there are enough retina scanners to store information about every person's retinas

(D) the number of blood vessels in the human retina is invariant, although the patterns they form differ from person to person

(E) there is no person whose retinas have been scanned by two or more different retina scanners

13. There are just two ways a moon could have been formed from the planet around which it travels: either part of the planet's outer shell spun off into orbit around the planet or else a large object, such as a comet or meteoroid, struck the planet so violently that it dislodged a mass of material from inside the planet. Earth's moon consists primarily of materials different from those of the Earth's outer shell.

If the statements above are true, which one of the following, if also true, would most help to justify drawing the conclusion that Earth's moon was not formed from a piece of the Earth?

(A) The moons of some planets in Earth's solar system were not formed primarily from the planets' outer shells.

(B) Earth's moon consists primarily of elements that differ from those inside the Earth.

(C) Earth's gravity cannot have trapped a meteoroid and pulled it into its orbit as the Moon.

(D) The craters on the surface of Earth's moon show that it has been struck by many thousands of large meteoroids.

(E) Comets and large meteoroids normally move at very high speeds.

14. Caffeine can kill or inhibit the growth of the larvae of several species of insects. One recent experiment showed that tobacco hornworm larvae die when they ingest a preparation that consists, in part, of finely powdered tea leaves, which contain caffeine. This result is evidence for the hypothesis that the presence of non-negligible quantities of caffeine in various parts of many diverse species of plants is not accidental but evolved as a defense for those plants.

The argument assumes that

(A) caffeine-producing plants are an important raw material in the manufacture of commercial insecticides

(B) caffeine is stored in leaves and other parts of caffeine-producing plants in concentrations roughly equal to the caffeine concentration of the preparation fed to the tobacco hornworm larvae

(C) caffeine-producing plants grow wherever insect larvae pose a major threat to indigenous plants or once posed a major threat to the ancestors of those plants

(D) the tobacco plant is among the plant species that produce caffeine for their own defense

(E) caffeine-producing plants or their ancestors have at some time been subject to being fed upon by creatures sensitive to caffeine

15. The only plants in the garden were tulips, but they were tall tulips. So the only plants in the garden were tall plants.

Which one of the following exhibits faulty reasoning most similar to the faulty reasoning in the argument above?

(A) The only dogs in the show were poodles, and they were all black poodles. So all the dogs in the show were black.

(B) All the buildings on the block were tall. The only buildings on the block were office buildings and residential towers. So all the office buildings on the block were tall buildings.

(C) All the primates in the zoo were gorillas. The only gorillas in the zoo were small gorillas. Thus the only primates in the zoo were small primates.

(D) The only fruit in the kitchen was pears, but the pears were not ripe. Thus none of the fruit in the kitchen was ripe.

(E) All the grand pianos here are large. All the grand pianos here are heavy. Thus everything large is heavy.

GO ON TO THE NEXT PAGE.

16. Scientific research will be properly channeled whenever those who decide which research to fund give due weight to the scientific merits of all proposed research. But when government agencies control these funding decisions, political considerations play a major role in determining which research will be funded, and whenever political considerations play such a role, the inevitable result is that scientific research is not properly channeled.

Which one of the following can be properly inferred from the statements above?

(A) There is no proper role for political considerations to play in determining who will decide which scientific research to fund.

(B) It is inevitable that considerations of scientific merit will be neglected in decisions regarding the funding of scientific research.

(C) Giving political considerations a major role in determining which scientific research to fund is incompatible with giving proper weight to the scientific merits of proposed research.

(D) When scientific research is not properly channeled, governments tend to step in and take control of the process of choosing which research to fund.

(E) If a government does not control investment in basic scientific research, political consideration will inevitably be neglected in deciding which research to fund.

17. A new silencing device for domestic appliances operates by producing sound waves that cancel out the sound waves produced by the appliance. The device, unlike conventional silencers, actively eliminates the noise the appliance makes, and for that reason vacuum cleaners designed to incorporate the new device will operate with much lower electricity consumption than conventional vacuum cleaners.

Which one of the following, if true, most helps to explain why the new silencing device will make lower electricity consumption possible?

(A) Designers of vacuum cleaner motors typically have to compromise the motors' efficiency in order to reduce noise production.

(B) The device runs on electricity drawn from the appliance's main power supply.

(C) Conventional vacuum cleaners often use spinning brushes to loosen dirt in addition to using suction to remove dirt.

(D) Governmental standards for such domestic appliances as vacuum cleaners allow higher electricity consumption when vacuum cleaners are quieter.

(E) The need to incorporate silencers in conventional vacuum cleaners makes them heavier and less mobile than they might otherwise be.

18. Because dinosaurs were reptiles, scientists once assumed that, like all reptiles alive today, dinosaurs were cold-blooded. The recent discovery of dinosaur fossils in the northern arctic, however, has led a number of researchers to conclude that at least some dinosaurs might have been warm-blooded. These researchers point out that only warm-blooded animals could have withstood the frigid temperatures that are characteristic of arctic winters, whereas cold-blooded animals would have frozen to death in the extreme cold.

Which one of the following, if true, weakens the researchers' argument?

(A) Today's reptiles are generally confined to regions of temperate or even tropical climates.

(B) The fossils show the arctic dinosaurs to have been substantially smaller than other known species of dinosaurs.

(C) The arctic dinosaur fossils were found alongside fossils of plants known for their ability to withstand extremely cold temperatures.

(D) The number of fossils found together indicates herds of dinosaurs so large that they would need to migrate to find a continual food supply.

(E) Experts on prehistoric climatic conditions believe that winter temperatures in the prehistoric northern arctic were not significantly different from what they are today.

GO ON TO THE NEXT PAGE.

90

Questions 19–20

Maria: Calling any state totalitarian is misleading: it implies total state control of all aspects of life. The real world contains no political entity exercising literally total control over even one such aspect. This is because any system of control is inefficient, and, therefore, its degree of control is partial.

James: A one-party state that has tried to exercise control over most aspects of a society and that has, broadly speaking, managed to do so is totalitarian. Such a system's practical inefficiencies do not limit the aptness of the term, which does not describe a state's actual degree of control as much as it describes the nature of a state's ambitions.

19. Which one of the following most accurately expresses Maria's main conclusion?

   (A)   No state can be called totalitarian without inviting a mistaken belief.
   (B)   To be totalitarian, a state must totally control society.
   (C)   The degree of control exercised by a state is necessarily partial.
   (D)   No existing state currently has even one aspect of society under total control.
   (E)   Systems of control are inevitably inefficient.

20. James responds to Maria's argument by

   (A)   pointing out a logical inconsistency between two statements she makes in support of her argument
   (B)   offering an alternative explanation for political conditions she mentions
   (C)   rejecting some of the evidence she presents without challenging what she infers from it
   (D)   disputing the conditions under which a key term of her argument can be appropriately applied
   (E)   demonstrating that her own premises lead to a conclusion different from hers

21. The similarity between ichthyosaurs and fish is an example of convergence, a process by which different classes of organisms adapt to the same environment by independently developing one or more similar external body features. Ichthyosaurs were marine reptiles and thus do not belong to the same class of organisms as fish. However, ichthyosaurs adapted to their marine environment by converging on external body features similar to those of fish. Most strikingly, ichthyosaurs, like fish, had fins.

If the statements above are true, which one of the following is an inference that can be properly drawn on the basis of them?

   (A)   The members of a single class of organisms that inhabit the same environment must be identical in all their external body features.
   (B)   The members of a single class of organisms must exhibit one or more similar external body features that differentiate that class from all other classes of organisms.
   (C)   It is only as a result of adaptation to similar environments that one class of organisms develops external body features similar to those of another class of organisms.
   (D)   An organism does not necessarily belong to a class simply because the organism has one or more external body features similar to those of members of that class.
   (E)   Whenever two classes of organisms share the same environment, members of one class will differ from members of the other class in several external body features.

GO ON TO THE NEXT PAGE.

22. Further evidence bearing on Jamison's activities must have come to light. On the basis of previously available evidence alone, it would have been impossible to prove that Jamison was a party to the fraud, and Jamison's active involvement in the fraud has now been definitively established.

The pattern of reasoning exhibited in the argument above most closely parallels that exhibited in which one of the following?

(A) Smith must not have purchased his house within the last year. He is listed as the owner of that house on the old list of property owners, and anyone on the old list could not have purchased his or her property within the last year.

(B) Turner must not have taken her usual train to Nantes today. Had she done so, she could not have been in Nantes until this afternoon, but she was seen having coffee in Nantes at 11 o'clock this morning.

(C) Norris must have lied when she said that she had not authorized the investigation. There is no doubt that she did authorize it, and authorizing an investigation is not something anyone is likely to have forgotten.

(D) Waugh must have known that last night's class was canceled. Waugh was in the library yesterday, and it would have been impossible for anyone in the library not to have seen the cancellation notices.

(E) LaForte must have deeply resented being passed over for promotion. He maintains otherwise, but only someone who felt badly treated would have made the kind of remark LaForte made at yesterday's meeting.

23. Reporting on a civil war, a journalist encountered evidence that refugees were starving because the government would not permit food shipments to a rebel-held area. Government censors deleted all mention of the government's role in the starvation from the journalist's report, which had not implicated either nature or the rebels in the starvation. The journalist concluded that it was ethically permissible to file the censored report, because the journalist's news agency would precede it with the notice "Cleared by government censors."

Which one of the following ethical criteria, if valid, would serve to support the journalist's conclusion while placing the least constraint on the flow of reported information?

(A) It is ethical in general to report known facts but unethical to do so while omitting other known facts if the omitted facts would substantially alter an impression of a person or institution that would be congruent with the reported facts.

(B) In a situation of conflict, it is ethical to report known facts and unethical to fail to report known facts that would tend to exonerate one party to the conflict.

(C) In a situation of censorship, it is unethical to make any report if the government represented by the censor deletes from the report material unfavorable to that government.

(D) It is ethical in general to report known facts but unethical to make a report in a situation of censorship if relevant facts have been deleted by the censor, unless the recipient of the report is warned that censorship existed.

(E) Although it is ethical in general to report known facts, it is unethical to make a report from which a censor has deleted relevant facts, unless the recipient of the report is warned that there was censorship and the reported facts do not by themselves give a misleading impression.

GO ON TO THE NEXT PAGE.

24. A birth is more likely to be difficult when the mother is over the age of 40 than when she is younger. Regardless of the mother's age, a person whose birth was difficult is more likely to be ambidextrous than is a person whose birth was not difficult. Since other causes of ambidexterity are not related to the mother's age, there must be more ambidextrous people who were born to women over 40 than there are ambidextrous people who were born to younger women.

The argument is most vulnerable to which one of the following criticisms?

(A) It assumes what it sets out to establish.
(B) It overlooks the possibility that fewer children are born to women over 40 than to women under 40.
(C) It fails to specify what percentage of people in the population as a whole are ambidextrous.
(D) It does not state how old a child must be before its handedness can be determined.
(E) It neglects to explain how difficulties during birth can result in a child's ambidexterity.

Questions 25–26

The government has no right to tax earnings from labor. Taxation of this kind requires the laborer to devote a certain percentage of hours worked to earning money for the government. Thus, such taxation forces the laborer to work, in part, for another's purpose. Since involuntary servitude can be defined as forced work for another's purpose, just as involuntary servitude is pernicious, so is taxing earnings from labor.

25. The argument uses which one of the following argumentative techniques?

(A) deriving a general principle about the rights of individuals from a judgment concerning the obligations of governments
(B) inferring what will be the case merely from a description of what once was the case
(C) inferring that since two institutions are similar in one respect, they are similar in another respect
(D) citing the authority of an economic theory in order to justify a moral principle
(E) presupposing the inevitability of a hierarchical class system in order to oppose a given economic practice

26. Which one of the following is an error of reasoning committed by the argument?

(A) It ignores a difference in how the idea of forced work for another's purpose applies to the two cases.
(B) It does not take into account the fact that labor is taxed at different rates depending on income.
(C) It mistakenly assumes that all work is taxed.
(D) It ignores the fact that the government also taxes income from investment.
(E) It treats definitions as if they were matters of subjective opinion rather than objective facts about language.

S T O P

IF YOU FINISH BEFORE TIME IS CALLED, YOU MAY CHECK YOUR WORK ON THIS SECTION ONLY.
DO NOT WORK ON ANY OTHER SECTION IN THE TEST.

SECTION IV

Time—35 minutes

27 Questions

Directions: Each passage in this section is followed by a group of questions to be answered on the basis of what is stated or implied in the passage. For some of the questions, more than one of the choices could conceivably answer the question. However, you are to choose the best answer; that is, the response that most accurately and completely answers the question, and blacken the corresponding space on your answer sheet.

Three kinds of study have been performed on Byron. There is the biographical study—the very valuable examination of Byron's psychology and the events in his life; Escarpit's 1958 work is an example
(5) of this kind of study, and biographers to this day continue to speculate about Byron's life. Equally valuable is the study of Byron as a figure important in the history of ideas; Russell and Praz have written studies of this kind. Finally, there are
(10) studies that primarily consider Byron's poetry. Such literary studies are valuable, however, only when they avoid concentrating solely on analyzing the verbal shadings of Byron's poetry to the exclusion of any discussion of biographical considerations. A
(15) study with such a concentration would be of questionable value because Byron's poetry, for the most part, is simply not a poetry of subtle verbal meanings. Rather, on the whole, Byron's poems record the emotional pressure of certain moments
(20) in his life. I believe we cannot often read a poem of Byron's, as we often can one of Shakespeare's, without wondering what events or circumstances in his life prompted him to write it.

No doubt the fact that most of Byron's poems
(25) cannot be convincingly read as subtle verbal creations indicates that Byron is not a "great" poet. It must be admitted too that Byron's literary craftsmanship is irregular and often his temperament disrupts even his lax literary method
(30) (although the result, an absence of method, has a significant purpose: it functions as a rebuke to a cosmos that Byron feels he cannot understand). If Byron is not a "great" poet, his poetry is nonetheless of extraordinary interest to us because
(35) of the pleasure it gives us. Our main pleasure in reading Byron's poetry is the contact with a singular personality. Reading his work gives us illumination—self-understanding—after we have seen our weaknesses and aspirations mirrored in
(40) the personality we usually find in the poems. Anyone who thinks that this kind of illumination is not a genuine reason for reading a poet should think carefully about why we read Donne's sonnets. It is Byron and Byron's idea of himself that hold
(45) his work together (and that enthralled early-nineteenth-century Europe). Different characters speak in his poems, but finally it is usually he himself who is speaking: a far cry from the impersonal poet Keats. Byron's poetry alludes to
(50) Greek and Roman myth in the context of

contemporary affairs, but his work remains generally of a piece because of his close presence in the poetry. In sum, the poetry is a shrewd personal performance, and to shut out Byron the man is to
(55) fabricate a work of pseudocriticism.

1. Which one of the following titles best expresses the main idea of the passage?

   (A) An Absence of Method: Why Byron Is Not a "Great" Poet
   (B) Byron: The Recurring Presence in Byron's Poetry
   (C) Personality and Poetry: The Biographical Dimension of Nineteenth-Century Poetry
   (D) Byron's Poetry: Its Influence on the Imagination of Early-Nineteenth-Century Europe
   (E) Verbal Shadings: The Fatal Flaw of Twentieth-Century Literary Criticism

2. The author's mention of Russell and Praz serves primarily to

   (A) differentiate them from one another
   (B) contrast their conclusions about Byron with those of Escarpit
   (C) point out the writers whose studies suggest a new direction for Byron scholarship
   (D) provide examples of writers who have written one kind of study of Byron
   (E) give credit to the writers who have composed the best studies of Byron

GO ON TO THE NEXT PAGE.

94

3. Which one of the following would the author most likely consider to be a valuable study of Byron?

(A) a study that compared Byron's poetic style with Keats' poetic style
(B) a study that argued that Byron's thought ought not to be analyzed in terms of its importance in the history of ideas
(C) a study that sought to identify the emotions felt by Byron at a particular time in his life
(D) a study in which a literary critic argues that the language of Byron's poetry was more subtle than that of Keats' poetry
(E) a study in which a literary critic drew on experiences from his or her own life

4. Which one of the following statements best describes the organization of the first paragraph of the passage?

(A) A generalization is made and then gradually refuted.
(B) A number of theories are discussed and then the author chooses the most convincing one.
(C) Several categories are mentioned and then one category is discussed in some detail.
(D) A historical trend is delineated and then a prediction about the future of the trend is offered.
(E) A classification is made and then a rival classification is substituted in its place.

5. The author mentions that "Byron's literary craftsmanship is irregular" (lines 27–28) most probably in order to

(A) contrast Byron's poetic skill with that of Shakespeare
(B) dismiss craftsmanship as a standard by which to judge poets
(C) offer another reason why Byron is not a "great" poet
(D) point out a negative consequence of Byron's belief that the cosmos is incomprehensible
(E) indicate the most-often-cited explanation of why Byron's poetry lacks subtle verbal nuances

6. According to the author, Shakespeare's poems differ from Byron's in that Shakespeare's poems

(A) have elicited a wider variety of responses from both literary critics and biographers
(B) are on the whole less susceptible to being read as subtle verbal creations
(C) do not grow out of, or are not motivated by, actual events or circumstances in the poet's life
(D) provide the attentive reader with a greater degree of illumination concerning his or her own weaknesses and aspirations
(E) can often be read without the reader's being curious about what biographical factors motivated the poet to write them

7. The author indicates which one of the following about biographers' speculation concerning Byron's life?

(A) Such speculation began in earnest with Escarpit's study.
(B) Such speculation continues today.
(C) Such speculation is less important than consideration of Byron's poetry.
(D) Such speculation has not given us a satisfactory sense of Byron's life.
(E) Such speculation has been carried out despite the objections of literary critics.

8. The passage supplies specific information that provides a definitive answer to which one of the following questions?

(A) What does the author consider to be the primary enjoyment derived from reading Byron?
(B) Who among literary critics has primarily studied Byron's poems?
(C) Which moments in Byron's life exerted the greatest pressure on his poetry?
(D) Has Byron ever been considered to be a "great" poet?
(E) Did Byron exert an influence on Europeans in the latter part of the nineteenth century?

GO ON TO THE NEXT PAGE.

The United States Supreme Court has not always resolved legal issues of concern to Native Americans in a manner that has pleased the Indian nations. Many of the Court's decisions have been
(5) products of political compromise that looked more to the temper of the times than to enduring principles of law. But accommodation is part of the judicial system in the United States, and judicial decisions must be assessed with this fact in mind.
(10) Despite the "accommodating" nature of the judicial system, it is worth noting that the power of the Supreme Court has been exercised in a manner that has usually been beneficial to Native Americans, at least on minor issues, and has not
(15) been wholly detrimental on the larger, more important issues. Certainly there have been decisions that cast doubt on the validity of this assertion. Some critics point to the patronizing tone of many Court opinions and the apparent rejection
(20) of Native American values as important points to consider when reviewing a case. However, the validity of the assertion can be illustrated by reference to two important contributions that have resulted from the exercise of judicial power.
(25) First, the Court has created rules of judicial construction that, in general, favor the rights of Native American litigants. The Court's attitude has been conditioned by recognition of the distinct disadvantages Native Americans faced when
(30) dealing with settlers in the past. Treaties were inevitably written in English for the benefit of their authors, whereas tribal leaders were accustomed to making treaties without any written account, on the strength of mutual promises sealed by religious
(35) commitment and individual integrity. The written treaties were often broken, and Native Americans were confronted with fraud and political and military aggression. The Court recognizes that past unfairness to Native Americans cannot be
(40) sanctioned by the force of law. Therefore, ambiguities in treaties are to be interpreted in favor of the Native American claimants, treaties are to be interpreted as the Native Americans would have understood them, and, under the reserved rights
(45) doctrine, treaties reserve to Native Americans all rights that have not been specifically granted away in other treaties.
A second achievement of the judicial system is the protection that has been provided against
(50) encroachment by the states into tribal affairs. Federal judges are not inclined to view favorably efforts to extend states' powers and jurisdictions because of the direct threat that such expansion poses to the exercise of federal powers. In the
(55) absence of a federal statute directly and clearly allocating a function to the states, federal judges are inclined to reserve for the federal government—and the tribal governments under its charge—all those powers and rights they can be said to have
(60) possessed historically.

9. According to the passage, one reason why the United States Supreme Court "has not always resolved legal issues of concern to Native Americans in a manner that has pleased the Indian nations" (lines 1–4) is that

(A) Native Americans have been prevented from presenting their concerns persuasively
(B) the Court has failed to recognize that the Indian nations' concerns are different from those of other groups or from those of the federal government
(C) the Court has been reluctant to curtail the powers of the federal government
(D) Native Americans faced distinct disadvantages in dealing with settlers in the past
(E) the Court has made political compromises in deciding some cases

10. It can be inferred that the objections raised by the critics mentioned in line 18 would be most clearly answered by a United States Supreme Court decision that

(A) demonstrated respect for Native Americans and the principles and qualities they consider important
(B) protected the rights of the states in conflicts with the federal government
(C) demonstrated recognition of the unfair treatment Native Americans received in the past
(D) reflected consideration of the hardships suffered by Native Americans because of unfair treaties
(E) prevented repetition of inequities experienced by Native Americans in the past

GO ON TO THE NEXT PAGE.

11. It can be inferred that the author calls the judicial system of the United States "accommodating" (line 10) primarily in order to

    (A) suggest that the decisions of the United States Supreme Court have been less favorable to Native Americans than most people believe
    (B) suggest that the United States Supreme Court should be more supportive of the goals of Native Americans
    (C) suggest a reason why the decisions of the United States Supreme Court have not always favored Native Americans
    (D) indicate that the United States Supreme Court has made creditable efforts to recognize the values of Native Americans
    (E) indicate that the United States Supreme Court attempts to be fair to all parties to a case

12. The author's attitude toward the United States Supreme Court's resolution of legal issues of concern to Native Americans can best be described as one of

    (A) wholehearted endorsement
    (B) restrained appreciation
    (C) detached objectivity
    (D) cautious opposition
    (E) suppressed exasperation

13. It can be inferred that the author believes that the extension of the states' powers and jurisdictions with respect to Native American affairs would be

    (A) possible only with the consent of the Indian nations
    (B) favorably viewed by the United States Supreme Court
    (C) in the best interests of both state and federal governments
    (D) detrimental to the interests of Native Americans
    (E) discouraged by most federal judges in spite of legal precedents supporting the extension

14. The author's primary purpose is to

    (A) contrast opposing views
    (B) reevaluate traditional beliefs
    (C) reconcile divergent opinions
    (D) assess the claims made by disputants
    (E) provide evidence to support a contention

15. It can be inferred that the author believes the United States Supreme Court's treatment of Native Americans to have been

    (A) irreproachable on legal grounds
    (B) reasonably supportive in most situations
    (C) guided by enduring principles of law
    (D) misguided but generally harmless
    (E) harmful only in a few minor cases

GO ON TO THE NEXT PAGE.

When catastrophe strikes, analysts typically
blame some combination of powerful mechanisms.
An earthquake is traced to an immense instability
along a fault line; a stock market crash is blamed on
(5)　the destabilizing effect of computer trading. These
explanations may well be correct. But systems as
large and complicated as the Earth's crust or the
stock market can break down not only under the
force of a mighty blow but also at the drop of a pin.
(10)　In a large interactive system, a minor event can start
a chain reaction that leads to a catastrophe.

　　Traditionally, investigators have analyzed large
interactive systems in the same way they analyze
small orderly systems, mainly because the methods
(15)　developed for small systems have proved so
successful. They believed they could predict the
behavior of a large interactive system by studying its
elements separately and by analyzing its component
mechanisms individually. For lack of a better
(20)　theory, they assumed that in large interactive
systems the response to a disturbance is
proportional to that disturbance.

　　During the past few decades, however, it has
become increasingly apparent that many large
(25)　complicated systems do not yield to traditional
analysis. Consequently, theorists have proposed a
"theory of self-organized criticality": many large
interactive systems evolve naturally to a critical
state in which a minor event starts a chain reaction
(30)　that can affect any number of elements in the
system. Although such systems produce more minor
events than catastrophes, the mechanism that leads
to minor events is the same one that leads to major
events.

(35)　　A deceptively simple system serves as a
paradigm for self-organized criticality: a pile of
sand. As sand is poured one grain at a time onto a
flat disk, the grains at first stay close to the position
where they land. Soon they rest on top of one
(40)　another, creating a pile that has a gentle slope. Now
and then, when the slope becomes too steep, the
grains slide down, causing a small avalanche. The
system reaches its critical state when the amount of
sand added is balanced, on average, by the amount
(45)　falling off the edge of the disk.

　　Now when a grain of sand is added, it can start
an avalanche of any size, including a "catastrophic"
event. Most of the time the grain will fall so that no
avalanche occurs. By studying a specific area of the
(50)　pile, one can even predict whether avalanches will
occur there in the near future. To such a local
observer, however, large avalanches would remain
unpredictable because they are a consequence of
the total history of the entire pile. No matter what
(55)　the local dynamics are, catastrophic avalanches
would persist at a relative frequency that cannot be
altered. Criticality is a global property of the
sandpile.

16. The passage provides support for all of the following
generalizations about large interactive systems
EXCEPT:

(A) They can evolve to a critical state.
(B) They do not always yield to traditional
analysis.
(C) They make it impossible for observers to make
any predictions about them.
(D) They are subject to the effects of chain
reactions.
(E) They are subject to more minor events than
major events.

17. According to the passage, the criticality of a sandpile
is determined by the

(A) size of the grains of sand added to the sandpile
(B) number of grains of sand the sandpile contains
(C) rate at which sand is added to the sandpile
(D) shape of the surface on which the sandpile
rests
(E) balance between the amount of sand added to
and the amount lost from the sandpile

GO ON TO THE NEXT PAGE.

98

18. It can be inferred from the passage that the theory employed by the investigators mentioned in the second paragraph would lead one to predict that which one of the following would result from the addition of a grain of sand to a sandpile?

    (A) The grain of sand would never cause anything more than a minor disturbance.
    (B) The grain of sand would usually cause a minor disturbance, but would occasionally cause a small avalanche.
    (C) The grain of sand would usually cause either a minor disturbance or a small avalanche, but would occasionally cause a catastrophic event.
    (D) The grain of sand would usually cause a catastrophic event, but would occasionally cause only a small avalanche or an even more minor disturbance.
    (E) The grain of sand would invariably cause a catastrophic event.

19. Which one of the following best describes the organization of the passage?

    (A) A traditional procedure is described and its application to common situations is endorsed; its shortcomings in certain rare but critical circumstances are then revealed.
    (B) A common misconception is elaborated and its consequences are described; a detailed example of one of these consequences is then given.
    (C) A general principle is stated and supported by several examples; an exception to the rule is then considered and its importance evaluated.
    (D) A number of seemingly unrelated events are categorized; the underlying processes that connect them are then detailed.
    (E) A traditional method of analysis is discussed and the reasons for its adoption are explained; an alternative is then described and clarified by means of an example.

20. Which one of the following is most analogous to the method of analysis employed by the investigators mentioned in the second paragraph?

    (A) A pollster gathers a sample of voter preferences and on the basis of this information makes a prediction about the outcome of an election.
    (B) A historian examines the surviving documents detailing the history of a movement and from these documents reconstructs a chronology of the events that initiated the movement.
    (C) A meteorologist measures the rainfall over a certain period of the year and from this data calculates the total annual rainfall for the region.
    (D) A biologist observes the behavior of one species of insect and from these observations generalizes about the behavior of insects as a class.
    (E) An engineer analyzes the stability of each structural element of a bridge and from these analyses draws a conclusion about the structural soundness of the bridge.

21. In the passage, the author is primarily concerned with

    (A) arguing against the abandonment of a traditional approach
    (B) describing the evolution of a radical theory
    (C) reconciling conflicting points of view
    (D) illustrating the superiority of a new theoretical approach
    (E) advocating the reconsideration of an unfashionable explanation

GO ON TO THE NEXT PAGE.

Historians have long accepted the notion that women of English descent who lived in the English colonies of North America during the seventeenth and eighteenth centuries were better off than either (5) the contemporary women in England or the colonists' own nineteenth-century daughters and granddaughters. The "golden age" theory originated in the 1920s with the work of Elizabeth Dexter, who argued that there were relatively few (10) women among the colonists, and that all hands—male and female—were needed to sustain the growing settlements. Rigid sex-role distinctions could not exist under such circumstances; female colonists could accordingly engage in whatever (15) occupations they wished, encountering few legal or social constraints if they sought employment outside the home. The surplus of male colonists also gave women crucial bargaining power in the marriage market, since women's contributions were vital to (20) the survival of colonial households.

Dexter's portrait of female colonists living under conditions of rough equality with their male counterparts was eventually incorporated into studies of nineteenth-century middle-class women. (25) The contrast between the self-sufficient colonial woman and the oppressed nineteenth-century woman, confined to her home by stultifying ideologies of domesticity and by the fact that industrialization eliminated employment (30) opportunities for middle-class women, gained an extraordinarily tenacious hold on historians. Even scholars who have questioned the "golden age" view of colonial women's status have continued to accept the paradigm of a nineteenth-century (35) decline from a more desirable past. For example, Joan Hoff-Wilson asserted that there was no "golden age" and yet emphasized that the nineteenth century brought "increased loss of function and authentic status for" middle-class (40) women.

Recent publications about colonial women have exposed the concept of a decline in status as simplistic and unsophisticated, a theory that based its assessment of colonial women's status solely on (45) one factor (their economic function in society) and assumed all too readily that a relatively simple social system automatically brought higher standing to colonial women. The new scholarship presents a far more complicated picture, one in which (50) definitions of gender roles, the colonial economy, demographic patterns, religion, the law, and household organization all contributed to defining the circumstances of colonial women's lives. Indeed, the primary concern of modern scholarship is not to (55) generalize about women's status but to identify the specific changes and continuities in women's lives during the colonial period. For example, whereas earlier historians suggested that there was little change for colonial women before 1800, the new (60) scholarship suggests that a three-part chronological division more accurately reflects colonial women's experiences. First was the initial period of English colonization (from the 1620s to about 1660); then a period during which patterns of family and (65) community were challenged and reshaped (roughly from 1660 to 1750); and finally the era of revolution (approximately 1750 to 1815), which brought other changes to women's lives.

22. Which one of the following best expresses the main idea of the passage?

(A) An earlier theory about the status of middle-class women in the nineteenth century has been supported by recent scholarship.
(B) Recent studies of middle-class nineteenth-century women have altered an earlier theory about the status of colonial women.
(C) Recent scholarship has exposed an earlier theory about the status of colonial women as too narrowly based and oversimplified.
(D) An earlier theory about colonial women has greatly influenced recent studies on middle-class women in the nineteenth century.
(E) An earlier study of middle-class women was based on insufficient research on the status of women in the nineteenth century.

23. The author discusses Hoff-Wilson primarily in order to

(A) describe how Dexter's theory was refuted by historians of nineteenth-century North America
(B) describe how the theory of middle-class women's nineteenth-century decline in status was developed
(C) describe an important influence on recent scholarship about the colonial period
(D) demonstrate the persistent influence of the "golden age" theory
(E) provide an example of current research on the colonial period

24. It can be inferred from the passage that the author would be most likely to describe the views of the scholars mentioned in line 32 as

(A) unassailable
(B) innovative
(C) paradoxical
(D) overly sophisticated
(E) without merit

GO ON TO THE NEXT PAGE.

25. It can be inferred from the passage that, in proposing the "three-part chronological division" (lines 60–61), scholars recognized which one of the following?

(A) The circumstances of colonial women's lives were defined by a broad variety of social and economic factors.
(B) Women's lives in the English colonies of North America were similar to women's lives in seventeenth- and eighteenth-century England.
(C) Colonial women's status was adversely affected when patterns of family and community were established in the late seventeenth century.
(D) Colonial women's status should be assessed primarily on the basis of their economic function in society.
(E) Colonial women's status was low when the colonies were settled but changed significantly during the era of revolution.

26. According to the author, the publications about colonial women mentioned in the third paragraph had which one of the following effects?

(A) They undermined Dexter's argument on the status of women colonists during the colonial period.
(B) They revealed the tenacity of the "golden age" theory in American history.
(C) They provided support for historians, such as Hoff-Wilson, who study the nineteenth century.
(D) They established that women's status did not change significantly from the colonial period to the nineteenth century.
(E) They provided support for earlier theories about women colonists in the English colonies of North America.

27. Practitioners of the new scholarship discussed in the last paragraph would be most likely to agree with which one of the following statements about Dexter's argument?

(A) It makes the assumption that women's status is determined primarily by their political power in society.
(B) It makes the assumption that a less complex social system necessarily confers higher status on women.
(C) It is based on inadequate research on women's economic role in the colonies.
(D) It places too much emphasis on the way definitions of gender roles affected women colonists in the colonial period.
(E) It accurately describes the way women's status declined in the nineteenth century.

S T O P

IF YOU FINISH BEFORE TIME IS CALLED, YOU MAY CHECK YOUR WORK ON THIS SECTION ONLY.
DO NOT WORK ON ANY OTHER SECTION IN THE TEST.

Directions:

1. Use the Answer Key on the next page to check your answers.

2. Use the Scoring Worksheet below to compute your raw score.

3. Use the Score Conversion Chart to convert your raw score into the 120-180 scale.

Scoring Worksheet

1. Enter the number of questions you answered correctly in each section.

	Number Correct
SECTION I	_____
SECTION II	_____
SECTION III	_____
SECTION IV	_____

2. Enter the sum here: _____
   This is your Raw Score.

Conversion Chart

For Converting Raw Score to the 120-180 LSAT Scaled Score
LSAT Form 4LSS25

Reported Score	Raw Score Lowest	Raw Score Highest
180	98	101
179	97	97
178	96	96
177	95	95
176	94	94
175	93	93
174	92	92
173	90	91
172	89	89
171	88	88
170	87	87
169	86	86
168	84	85
167	83	83
166	82	82
165	80	81
164	79	79
163	77	78
162	76	76
161	74	75
160	73	73
159	71	72
158	69	70
157	68	68
156	66	67
155	65	65
154	63	64
153	61	62
152	60	60
151	58	59
150	56	57
149	55	55
148	53	54
147	51	52
146	50	50
145	48	49
144	46	47
143	45	45
142	43	44
141	42	42
140	40	41
139	39	39
138	37	38
137	36	36
136	34	35
135	33	33
134	31	32
133	30	30
132	29	29
131	27	28
130	26	26
129	25	25
128	24	24
127	23	23
126	22	22
125	21	21
124	20	20
123	18	19
122	17	17
121	_*	_*
120	0	16

*There is no raw score that will produce this scaled score for this form.

LSAT WRITING SAMPLE TOPIC

Zelmar Corporation, an advertising company, must move its offices from their current downtown location. The company is considering an alternate building downtown and a suburban location. Write an argument favoring one of these choices over the other based on the following considerations:

- Zelmar wants as many employees as possible to remain with the company.
- Due to recent financial setbacks, Zelmar wants to make the coming year as profitable as possible.

The downtown location is in a somewhat smaller building a few blocks away from Zelmar's current offices and within the general area where a large proportion of the company's clients have offices. Rental costs would be slightly lower than those of its current location. Near a subway stop and close to numerous shops and restaurants, the building is located one block from a day care center that promises discounts to Zelmar employees, many of whom have preschool children. Because of space restrictions, about half of Zelmar's employees would have to give up their offices and work in a large open area subdivided by portable walls.

The suburban location is twenty miles from downtown, and the commute for many employees would at least double. While there is ample free parking, the subway line does not extend to this location; there is a bus stop directly outside the building. Zelmar would pay far less in rent than it currently does, and most employees could have their own offices. Located in an office park complex, this building has excellent facilities for large meetings and ample space for Zelmar to expand its business. A large cafeteria in the building offers food from 7 A.M. until 6 P.M. at a cost considerably below that of commercial restaurants. Employees from other offices have proposed a day care center to serve the entire complex.

SECTION I

1.	D	8.	B	15.	A	22.	C
2.	E	9.	C	16.	A	23.	A
3.	A	10.	E	17.	E	24.	C
4.	E	11.	C	18.	A		
5.	C	12.	B	19.	D		
6.	D	13.	D	20.	E		
7.	E	14.	B	21.	A		

SECTION II

1.	B	8.	E	15.	E	22.	E
2.	A	9.	C	16.	E	23.	E
3.	D	10.	E	17.	B	24.	E
4.	E	11.	D	18.	A		
5.	C	12.	B	19.	A		
6.	D	13.	D	20.	E		
7.	C	14.	D	21.	A		

SECTION III

1.	D	8.	B	15.	C	22.	B
2.	B	9.	A	16.	C	23.	D
3.	B	10.	A	17.	A	24.	B
4.	C	11.	E	18.	D	25.	C
5.	D	12.	A	19.	A	26.	A
6.	C	13.	B	20.	D		
7.	A	14.	E	21.	D		

SECTION IV

1.	B	8.	A	15.	B	22.	C
2.	D	9.	E	16.	C	23.	D
3.	C	10.	A	17.	E	24.	C
4.	C	11.	C	18.	A	25.	A
5.	C	12.	B	19.	E	26.	A
6.	E	13.	D	20.	E	27.	B
7.	B	14.	E	21.	D		

Answer Explanations

Section 1

1. D: The puzzle assigns 8 students to three classes, and we know there are three students in the first two classes and two in the third. The first rule states R must be in the first class. All five choices adhere to this, so we have not ruled any out and can move on to the second rule. This rule states that S must be in class 3. Here, we find that Choice *B* can be eliminated because it incorrectly places S in class 2. In rule 3: Neither S nor W can be added to the same class as Y. We know that S needs to be in class 3, so then we can quickly scan and see that S is not paired with Y in any of the four choices we have left. When we check W, we find that in Choice *E,* W is with Y in class 2, so we can eliminate this choice. Rule 4 says that V cannot be added to the same class as Z. This occurs in Choice *C,* so that choice is incorrect. We are left with Choices *A* and *D,* and we have one rule left: If T is added to class 1, Z must also be added to class 1. In Choice *A,* we see T in class 1 but Z is in class 3, so this lineup violates the rule. After eliminating it, we are left with Choice *D,* which is the only option that does not violate any of the conditions.

2. E: This question asks us to determine what restrictions are placed specifically on V. If we look at the rules, we see that only rule 4 (V cannot be added to the same class as Z) directly involves V. Looking a step further, because none of the rules dictate exactly which class Z is in (and thus that V could not be in), V can theoretically be in any of the three classes.

3. A: X must be in class 1, and we are asked to determine how this assignment would affect the other students. We know that R must be in class 1, according to the first rule. This would be problematic with the new constraints of adding X to class 1 because then we'd have 4 students (R (who must be there), X (added in this question), T and Z (according to the fifth rule)). Therefore, T cannot be in class 1. In this case, T would have to go to class 2 because class 3 can only accept two students. The second rule dictates that one of these be S. The third rule states that S can't be with Y and W cannot be with Y. That means that S and W would need to be together in class 3 so that Y could be in class 2 away from them since all the seats in class 1 were already allocated to other students. That means the two seats in class 3 are also taken (S and W), leaving only a seat in class 2 for T.

4. E: Now we are told to consider X in class 3 and we need to select the one answer choice that does *not* work—the one that violates a rule. Here again, we find that the last rule, combined with the third rule, places the strictest constraints on the players in the puzzle and indeed, T and Z cannot be a viable pair for class 1 in this instance. If X is in class 3 with S (according to the second rule), and T and Z and R are in class 1, that leaves V, W, and Y for class 2. This violates the third rule, however, because W and Y are incompatible.

5. C: If T is added to class 3, S and T are in class 3. W and Y must be separated, as must V and Z. We don't have specifics as to which member of each pair (W and Y or V and Z) must be in which class, but we do know that R is in class 1 (leaving two slots), so X must be in class 2, leaving two spots. If X was in class 1, there would only be one opening for one of the W/Y members *and* one of the V/Z members, but we obviously need two openings to accommodate one member of each incompatible pair. By moving X to class 2, both class 1 and 2 have two open slots to split up these pairs.

6. D: The most effective way to answer this question is to go through and test each option. Choice *A* says that V must be added to class 3 if T and X are added to class 2. While this can be possible, it doesn't have to be true. We know V can't be with Z, but if we put Z in class 2 with T and X and V in class 1 with R and Y, and S and W in class 3, no rules are violated. Choice *B* is incorrect because T can be added to class 2 without violating any rules. Choice *C* is incorrect because Z can be added to class 2. If V and X are added to class 1, we have class 1 full (R, V, and X). Since S is in class 3, Y has to be in class 2 because according to the third rule, S and Y cannot be together. W and Y also cannot be together as per this rule, which would force W to class 3 with S to separate them both safely from Y. Therefore, Choice *D* must be true. Choice *E* is incorrect because X could be added to class 1.

7. E: We have four lions and two tigers going into six stalls that are arranged in facing pairs. We know the two tigers can't be in a facing stalls), the lions are in stalls 1 and 6 (since H is a lion), and J cannot be the lion in stall 1 because rule 4 says J is in a stall numbered one higher than that of K. Accordingly, K cannot be in stalls 5 or 6 (H is in 6) and 5 would be the next highest but J needs to be one higher. Lastly, K cannot be in stall 3 because 3 faces H. That rule then tells us that J cannot be in 4 since J must be one higher than K. That leaves only stalls 2 or 4 as possible options for K. We are looking for the option that *must* be true and K must be in either stall 2 or 4 which is presented in *Choice E.*

8. B: Choice *A* states that F is in a stall one higher than J. We know from the last question, that J must be in stalls 3 or 5 because J is in a stall numbered one higher than K, and K must be in either stall 2 or 4. We know H is in 6, so if Choice *A* were true we'd have to place K in 2, J in 3, and F in 4 since the other option would push F to 6, but 6 is occupied. However, this would not work because M is forced to stall 5 by default (because stall 1 must be a lion so it's G). Stalls 2 and 5 face each other though and the first rule states that the two tigers cannot face one another. Thus, Choice *A* cannot be true. Let's check Choice *B*. Hypothetically, could H face M? We know H is in stall 6, so could M be in stall 3? M could be in stall 3 in the scenario where K is in 4 and J is in 5. Here, F or G could be in either stall 1 or 2. So far, this seems to work, but let's check the next option. We already know J must be in stall 3 or 5 because K is in 2 or 4. Choice *C* can be ruled out. Choice *D* can also be ruled out because K and J cannot face one another because no two consecutive stalls face one another and J and K are only to be one apart. Lastly, Choice *E* poses that K and J are in different rows. This could only be the case if they occupied stalls 3 and 4, as these are the only two consecutive stalls that bridge the two rows. However, K cannot be in stall 3 (as was determined in problem #7), so this option in invalid. Thus, Choice *B* is the only possibility.

9. C: It is clear from the various restrictions on the tigers (K and M) and what we've uncovered about the rules that Choice *C* must be true. Because there are lions in stalls 1 and 6, which are on the ends of different rows and one of the tigers (K) must be next to J (a lion) on either of these two rows (occupying stalls 2 and 3 in row 1 or stalls 4 and 5 in the other row), M would not have space to also inhabit the row with K as all 3 stalls are already accounted for. Therefore, the stalls for K and M must be in different rows. Some of the choices *could* be true but do not necessarily have to be true.

10. E: In this question, we are asked to consider what would happen if K and H are in the same row. We know that H is in stall 6 and we've already discovered that K an only be in stalls 2 or 4, which means off the bat, before even looking at the answer choices, we know if K and H are in the same row, K is in stall 4, J is in stall 5, and H is in 6. Choice *A* states that F and J would be in the same row. We know this isn't true because we just reviewed that the row with J is filled up with K, J, and H, leaving no room for F. This choice is incorrect. Choice *B* says F is in a lower-numbered stall than G. At quick glance, we don't have enough information worked out yet to rule out or prove Choices *B, C,* or *D*. However, Choice *E* can be identified as the correct choice using what we have already discerned. Because the second row is filled with K, J, and H, by default, G and M must be in the same row.

11. C: Choice *A* is incorrect because if J is in stall 3, we know K is in stall 2 as per the fourth rule. Choice *B* is incorrect because if F is in stall 4 and H is in stall 6 (rule 3), the only stall for the other tiger, M, is 5, but 5 is facing stall 2, which would be housing tiger K. M has to be in stall 4 if J is in 3 to keep the tigers out of stalls facing one another. This also makes Choice *E* incorrect. That leaves Choice *C,* where G is in stall 1, as the correct answer for a choice that could be true. If G is in stall 1, it fulfills the requirement for a lion in stall 1 per rule 1. Then we have K in 2, J in 3, M in 4, F would be in 5, and H in 6. This lineup does not violate any rules.

12. B: We know that because the two tigers cannot face each other and K must be in either stall 2 or 4, a tiger must always be in stall 4. When K is in stall 2, M must be in 4 to avoid being across from K in stall 5. Therefore, a tiger is always in stall 4.

13. D: We have eight houses of three styles and five rules. A diagram is a helpful place to start:

1	3 (R)	5 (*T)	7
2	4	6 (SL)	8

We are told that house 3 is a ranch and 6 is a split-level house per rules 4 and 5. Rule 1 says that adjacent houses are of different styles, and rule 2 says split-level houses cannot face one another. Therefore, house 5 must be a Tudor because it can't be a split-level home (as it's across from 6, which is a split-level house) and it can't be a ranch because it's adjacent to 3, which is a ranch. Therefore, we can answer the question with Choice *D:* house 7 cannot be a Tudor house because 5 must be a Tudor, and adjacent houses cannot be of the same style per rule 1.

14. B: If considering two ranch houses opposite one another, we have to return to our diagram and the rules. We already know houses 5 and 6 can't be the ranch pair. House 1 can't be a ranch because 3 is, so for this given problem, neither can house 2 since we need a viable opposite pair. The third rule dictates that every ranch home needs an adjacent Tudor, but house 8 is on the end, so it only has one adjacent neighbor, and the last rule tells us that that house (house 6) is a split-level home. We can update our diagram to reflect the new findings about house 8. It must be a Tudor house because it can't be a split-level home or ranch. Thus, Choice *A* is incorrect. It also means Choice *C* is incorrect because house 4 would have to be a ranch house so that at least one pair of opposite houses are ranches (no other opposite pairs are both free to be ranch style, and we are already told house 3 is a ranch). Because we just determined that house 4 must be a ranch house in this situation, house 2 would have to be a Tudor house in order to satisfy the third rule; consequently, Choice *D* is incorrect. Choice *E* is incorrect because house 3 is a ranch so house 1 (adjacent) cannot also be a ranch, as this would violate the first rule.

15. A: Let's update our diagram to temporarily make house 4 a Tudor house for this problem:

1	3 (R)	5 (T)	7
2	4 **(T)**	6 (SL)	8 (T)

Now, let's address the answer choices. Choice *A* states that 1 could be a Tudor. This seems plausible because it would not violate any rules. Just to be sure, we will look at the other choices. Choice *B* states that house 2 is a Tudor house. This can't be because 4 is a Tudor house in this problem, and as per the first rule, adjacent houses must be of different styles. Choice *C* is also incorrect because it has house 5 as a ranch, but we know for sure that 5 is a Tudor house. For the same reasoning as Choice *B*, Choice *D* is incorrect: because house 5 is a Tudor house, house 7 cannot be. Lastly, Choice *E* is incorrect because we determined it to be a Tudor house. Therefore, circling back, only Choice *A* is possible.

16. A: Here is another "could be" question, now considering all eight houses and their styles. The answer options include ranch houses and Tudor houses, so it initially appears that we will need to calculate the possible permutations for those house types to uncover the answer. However, there are a few options we can eliminate. Choice *E*, five ranch houses, is not possible because there would have to be at least two ranch houses adjacent to each other. Choice *B* can be immediately eliminated because we already know there are at least two Tudor houses (5 and 8). Let's consider if there *could* be just those 2 (Choice *C*). We would need to make house 1 a split-level house because we can't use any more Tudor homes without going over our "budget," and we already know house 1 cannot be a ranch due to its position next to house 3. House 2 would then be forced to be a ranch as we can't have two opposite split levels. If it is a ranch, house 4 would have to be a Tudor to satisfy the third rule. However, we can't have another Tudor house, so this choice is impossible. We are left with Choices *A* and *D*. Let's look at *D*, four ranches. This is a similar discussion to that for Choice *E*, except that we know we can have one non-ranch house in our 4 open houses. Since house 1 cannot be a ranch, every other house there that is unassigned (2, 4, and 7) would need to be ranches, but this will not work because houses 2 and 4 are adjacent. This leaves Choice *A* as the answer by default, but let's see if we can work out a permissible line up with one ranch; we already have one (house 3), which means no other homes can be of that style. Remember, we just need to find a workable assignment, not the definitive one. The following fulfills the requirements without violating any rules and includes only one ranch house:

1 (T)	3 (R)	5 (T)	7 (SL)
2 (SL)	4 (T)	6 (SL)	8 (T)

17. E: Given the rules that House 3 is a ranch house and House 6 is a split-level house and considering the stipulations of the question, house 4 would have to be a Tudor house; no adjacent home can be the same, and no same home can face each other. Because a ranch home is on one side of the street and a split-level home is on the opposite side and one space over, the only possible option is for a Tudor home. This is the only relevant answer choice and home that can be determined from the information that is provided. To assume anything else would be mere speculation and lead our logic astray. Choice *E* is correct.

18. A: Notice that only Choice *A* has house 2 as a ranch. Choices *B* and *C* are both split-levels, and Choices *D* and *E* are both Tudors. This is obviously not the only house to consider, but as it is the first house in the list and we are looking for the one impossible lineup, catching an immediate difference is favorable from an efficiency standpoint. Delving now into that first difference in Choice *A*, we should consider if house 2 could actually be a ranch. We quickly can determine that it cannot be a ranch when the next house in the lineup is listed as a split-level because every ranch has to have at least one Tudor next to it. Therefore, we know Choice *A* is unworkable and is thus the correct choice for this problem.

19. D: We have five ranked teams that start as R, J, S, M, L with R as 1 (the best) and the others numbered in order accordingly. In this question, just one round of even-matches has occurred, so we look to the third rule and see that teams in positions 2 and 4 play those immediately above that (1 and 3) in even rounds. Therefore, J played R and M played S. This means that team L did not play. Of the lineups given in the five choices, only Choice *D* appropriately leaves L in last place; we can select this choice for this reason.

20. E: We know an odd round occurred and then an even round. We are also told that the lower-positioned teams have won each matchup in both rounds in this scenario. Thus, for the first round, S played J and L played M, and S and L won. After that round, as per the rules, the order is now R, S, J, L, M. For the even round, S plays and beats R and L plays and beats J, so we have S, R, L, J, M. At this point, we can review our choices. We are looking for the one *false* statement. Choice *A* states that L is one better than J, which it is. So there is nothing wrong with that choice. Choice *B* states that R is one place better than L, which it is. Thus, we can rule out this choice. Choice *C* states that S is one place better than R, which it is, so again, we can rule out this choice. Choice *D* states that J is in position 4, which it is. Thus, we can rule out this choice. Finally, Choice *E* states that M is in position 3, which it is not. We have found our answer.

21. A: Starting this problem with an odd match, the sequence could change from R, J, S, M, L to R, J, S, L, M. Following this sequence with an even match, the final sequence would become: J, R, L, S, M. If you follow this pattern, you will find that J has won two matches, making Choice *A* a possible answer. In this case, L has won both matches; R has not played two matches to win; L did not play J; and M and S never played each other. Thus, Choice *A* is our best option. If you were to start with an even round, you would not come to a solution for this problem because J would only play one game; L would only play one game; R would have lost both matches; L still would not have played J; and M would only play S once. Because of this, we know we must start with an odd match and come to choose *A* as our answer.

22. C: Choices *A* and *B* can immediately be eliminated because J starts in second position and we are told J has won all of their matches, so they would have advanced to first, rather than stayed in second or dropped to third. On that note, we can eliminate Choice *D* since J would have assumed first place if they won all of their games; we are not told about R's performance. It is possible for L to be in position 2 after 3 rounds if they won all their games. Consider this:

R, J, S, M, L becomes R, J, S, L, M if an odd-round game is played first and they win.

Then, in the next even-round game (game #2), R, J, S, L, M becomes J, R, L, S, M.

Finally, in the third game, an odd-round game, if they win again J, R, L, S, M becomes J, L, R, M, S. L has jumped up to the second spot.

23. A: No matter which order the sequence is set up, whether odd-even-odd or even-odd-even, the results each end with M winning its three matches and J being in the third position. Because this is seen immediately after working through the problem, we know that Choice *A* is correct and that the other answer choices are irrelevant. Even-Odd-Even Sequencing: R, J, S, M, L **to** R, J, M, S, L **to** R, M, J, S, L **to** M, R J, S, L. Odd-Even-Odd Sequencing: R, J, S, M, L **to** R, J, S, M, L **to** R, J, M, S, L **to** R, M, J, S, L.

24. C: Choice *A* can be eliminated because M jumps to position 5 after round 3 from position 3 in this hypothetical second round, and a team can't jump two positions in a round. Choice *A* is out. In Choice *B,* R moves from position five to position one after the third round. This is not possible and therefore is the incorrect choice. Choice *C* does not seem to have any major gaps in position of teams. Choices *D* and *E* both have J in fifth whereas J ends up in second after round 3. Again, these movements are not possible and are therefore incorrect. Concluding that Choice *C* is our workable option.

Section 2

1. B: If a significant proportion of the racoon population became ill with rabies the year before last, then likely many racoons died and the population has dwindled. The city's disease control center is reporting that the percentage of infected racoons have increased, but this says nothing about the total number of cases. After all, 1 is 100% of 1 whereas 1 is 1% of 100.

2. A: Choice A negates the relevance of this contingency. A mouse is not a domesticated farm animal, so if the animal exclusion rule only pertains to farm animals, the reviewers' argument and patent denial is nullified. Choice B is fairly irrelevant; it should not matter how many similar patents the university has submitted. Choice C supports rather than weakens the argument.

Choice D is incorrect because the argument has nothing to do with plants nor do we know if there are similar restrictions on granting patents for developments that are considered new plant varieties. Lastly, Choice E somewhat weakens the argument but is incorrect because it does not say that "new" animals that are created via genetically-modified routes are exempt from the rule and that it only pertains to conventionally-derived species.

3. D: Choice *D* is stated nearly explicitly in the passage. It states that the water in all the municipalities considered here met the regional government's "standards for cleanliness", which presumably means they have considered a reasonably safe bacterial level and incorporated that into their going standards. There is no information in the passage to support Choices *A, C,* or *E.* We also cannot conclude that Choice *B* is true. While the argument reports that the water in deep aquifers does not contain any disease-causing bacteria specifically, there might be other bacteria contained within. We do not have enough information to conclude that there is "no bacteria of any kind."

4. E: If municipalities that do not chlorinate their water are subject to stricter regulations in regards to pipes and water tanks than those that do, it makes sense that the reason the water in municipalities that did not chlorinate their water had less bacterial contamination. The passage states that the contamination comes from flaws in pipes or storage tanks. Therefore, if fewer flaws are allowed, it makes sense that less bacteria would infiltrate and contaminate the water.

5. C: The argument makes sense in its rationale for the decrease in songbird population. However, if Choice *C* were to be true, the explanation becomes nullified: if there has been no change in the destructive, predatory magpie population in the actual area with the songbirds, then it's relatively unreasonable to justify the drop in songbirds with magpie action. Doing so would insinuate that the same number of magpies there have ramped up their egg and chick eating behaviors. We don't have any reason to believe that is the case. Therefore, because the magpie population hasn't changed in the songbird area, a major hole in the argument is uncovered. Choice *A* ultimately doesn't influence the argument either way; we are talking about "recent" years, which, presumably, should been captured in this window of the past 30 years of documentation. Choices *B* and *E* do weaken the argument somewhat, but neither are as strong of an answer in terms of their ability to dismantle the argument. Choice *D* actually strengthens the argument by providing a sound reason for a boom in the magpie population laid out in the initial argument as the ultimate culprit.

6. D: Choice *A* is incorrect because while it is true that part of the argument asserts that these markings were derived by humans and serve as the earliest evidence yet discovered of numerical representation, the crux of the argument is that it was that these ancient relics lacked systematic methods anyway, so it actually does not impact the argument either way.

7. C: Choice *C* most closely parallels the politician's flawed pattern of reasoning because both situations involve assuming that just because a seemingly logical cause for the observed problem (pollution or prison violence) was not present—and thus could not have contributed—to the existence of the problem as it previously occurred, it does not mean that such a cause (allowing the public access to the bay or criminals of violent crimes to mix with other prisoners) will not have any negative bearing or exacerbate the problem down the line. There can be multiple causes for any problem; it's certainly possible that the problems could get worse with the introduction of these risk factors.

8. E: The principle expressed is that humans get accustomed to certain conventions in products and that it's confusing—if not dangerous—when manufacturers sway from these expectations. A tape recorder that has a red "start" button, rather than green, and a yellow "stop" button, rather than red, exemplifies a deviation from the norm. Choices *A, B,* and *C* serve to further provide instances wherein conventions are upheld, so these are all incorrect. Choice *D* also just lists another convention.

9. C: If the total energy use over the years in question increased less than 10 percent but the electrical energy use over the same period increased by over 50 percent, then it follows that the proportion of electrical energy contributing to the total energy use increased during this time.

10. E: This argument fails to quantify the amount of "demeaning" work and in doing so, it does not consider whether the demeaning work eliminated by effective robots would be greater than the amount of demeaning work they may create. Each of the remaining answer choices really only address a definition for "demeaning work" rather than, as mentioned in choice *E,* addressing the potential gain with the incorporation of robots.

11. D: Choice *D* is correct through inference from what is suggested in the passage. The passage states the needles must be monitored by the sewing machine operators; it also states that it would be "inefficient" for factories to hire people solely to address worn needles with the new automated sewing operations. From these two pieces of information, the reader can infer that the needles "wear out at unpredictable rates". If it were consistent with how often needles wore out, factories could hire someone to come and fix them, but because it is unpredictable, they would be wasting money for someone to stand around, hoping a needle wore out. Each of the other answer options are either irrelevant or not inferable.

12. B: Theresa believes that the town's priority is the health of its citizens, while Alexander believes the priority is making right by the damage done to the local wildlife and forests. Theresa doesn't oppose the idea that the dump was potentially environmentally "disastrous," but she argues that *only if* it presents a human health hazard (what she considers top priority) should more money be allocated to fixing it.

13. D: Alexander believes the town has a duty to rectify the damage done to the local wildlife and forests by the installation of the chemical waste dump. Theresa would agree to cleaning up the waste dump if, and only if, it is posing a significant health risk to the town's citizens at this time. Even if the dump is environmentally "disastrous," she does not believe the town is responsible for redressing it at this time, as resources are limited and should be directed elsewhere as long as the risk to human health is currently spared. This is best summarized by Choice *D*.

14. D: The argument just states that the *difference* between Country A's per capita GDP and that of the European Economic Community increased to $6000, when adjusting for inflation, over that 10-year period. The use of the term "difference" should alert test takers to the lack of specificity in the argument. It is possible that instead of the European Economic Community's per capita GDP necessarily trending positive or staying stable, it could have decreased, or even plummeted precipitously. Say, for instance, in 1980, Country A's per capita GDP was $50,000; this would make the European Economic Community's $45,000 based on the first sentence. However, if after adjusting for inflation, in 1990, the European Economic Community's per capita GDP has dropped to $30,000, Country A's has dropped to $36,000, which still keeps a *difference* of $6000, but reflects a presumably lower standard of living in Country A (and the European Economic Community in general).

15. E: Choices *A, B,* and *C* would affect both private and municipal companies, so they can be eliminated. Choice *D* actually would provide a reason why municipal companies might be able to complete work faster than private companies, so it is not a good choice here. However, Choice *E* provides a reasonable justification for the discrepancy: if private companies can start getting supplies and working immediately, they avoid the lengthy holdup process experienced by municipal agencies.

16. E: The argument is that the population of sharks of a given species must have remained constant between the 1973 and current level because the CPUE has been consistent, but there are two components to consider when calculating CPUE: the population or number of sharks of a species in the waters to contribute to the count and the "per unit effort," which is a measure of how quickly and readily the sharks in the water can be counted. If the technology or process by which the same number of sharks in the water are counted improves, the rate of the count, and the "unit effort," would decrease. The introduction of sophisticated electronic location equipment, as described by Choice *E,* should theoretically hasten the counting process because it reportedly improves the locating ability. The other answer choices do little to affect the argument either way.

17. B: Ping's response questions the soundness of the solution Winston proposed by raising a point (the fact that many of those riders also ride the other way to work during peak hours, and cutting late-night hours would force these riders to seek alternative means of transport all together, meaning the PTA would lose their peak ride as well) that Winston failed to consider, or at least address. Ping exposes an overlooked—but relevant—hole in Winston's argument.

18. A: If it is true that over 23 percent of the round trips made by riders of the PTA include one leg during the late-night period, it stands to reason that removing the service offering of late-night rides will cause some of all of this population of riders to consider alternative means for *both* directions of the commute, since one will no longer be an option. Ping's conclusion is supported by this fact because it should be expected that some, if not most, of nearly a quarter of all roundtrip ridership will be lost when one of the two directions they travel is no longer possible.

19. A: Choice *A,* which, like the stimulus argument, proposes a single alternative to a current situation (Dominique taking the bus instead of walking, much like Dolores holding the director position instead of Victor), then provides a positive aspect to be gained by such a switch (the bus stops closer to her house), and ends with a negative aspect of the current situation that will be negated by the new solution (the subway doesn't go directly to the school, but the bus will; that walk in between will be avoided). None of the other options are crafted using this pattern of reasoning.

20. E: Choices *A* and *B* make a jump that we just don't have the evidence to support. We don't have ample evidence to say that the cause of that change on the income was from the high tuition paid by students from outside Markland. Choice *B* makes a hasty conclusion, so it is incorrect; there could be a variety of other factors that affect enrollment of non-local students, besides academic standards, that are not discussed. While Choice *C* looks appealing, we do not have enough information to say there are more or less students enrolling now than before in either group. The stimulus only tells us that the *proportions* of students have changed. There is not enough information to infer what is said in Choice *D*. Choice *E* is correct because it is the only answer choice that directly relates to what is being said in the question because as academic standards has risen, out of province attendance has decline, where one can infer that the number of inland attendance has increased so as to balance out the scale, so to speak (which can be inferred from the fact that tuition revenue has remained the same).

21. A: Variables, such as environmental factors (extreme weather, etc.) or changes in the forest that scientists may be unaware of, can be controlled for if indeed a subgroup of the species who are not affected by the fungus can be identified and set as the control group. Furthermore, the entomologists' conclusion would be supported, if, as stated in Choice *A,* the population of this subgroup increased their share of the total gypsy moth population because it indicates that there isn't another factor affecting the gypsy moths in general, regardless as to their reactivity to the fungus. Choice *B* is irrelevant to the entomologists' conclusion. Choices *C* and *D* would affect all gypsy moths unilaterally, regardless as to their reactivity to the fungus. Choice *E* does not control for other variables. It is possible that there are larger, more global factors that have affected the gypsy moths in a region like major storms or droughts, or perhaps the oak trees in the other forests unadulterated by the entomologists fell prey to the same fungus naturally.

22. E: Earlier on in the director of personnel's argument, he states: "[Ms. Tours] was denied merit raises to which she was entitled" and that she presented "compelling evidence that her job performance has been both excellent in itself and markedly superior to that of others who were awarded merit raises." Therefore, his concern that granting her a raise will now send an undesirable message to other employees that complaining, not merit, can earn you a raise is negated by his own admissions and assertions of Ms. Tours' merit-based deservedness of a raise, which abides by the company's policy.

23. D: T's response challenges S's claim that essentially says voting and fighting for one's country require the same maturity. Instead, T points out a reason he or she believes fighting and voting are inherently different because of the vastly different skillsets they require. Choice *A* is incorrect because T certainly doesn't say anything particularly supportive of S's argument. Choices *B* and *C* are wrong because T's response has nothing to do with distinguishing rights and obligations. Choice *E* is incorrect because T is just challenging S's claim, but not arguing that the voting and fighting age should necessarily be different, just that they have very different physical and mental requirements.

24. E: The passage makes the assumption that the Supreme Court must adhere to the standards of the Constitution. However, this premise isn't necessarily true. It is equally possible that the Supreme Court doesn't have to adhere strictly to the constitution. Choice *A* is incorrect because there was no data presented to support any claim. Choice *B* is incorrect because the passage never claims that this is a widely held view. Choice *C* is incorrect because there is no indication that anyone was going to profit from any decision that was made. Finally, Choice *D* is incorrect because there is no mention of the rights of individuals vs the rights of groups.

Section 3

1. D: Choice *D* weakens the argument the most because if the stickier webs are more visible to the spider's prey, the painted spiders may ultimately not be more successful as predators. In fact, the reflection of light that deters the insects may completely negate the benefit of the increased stickiness, or worse, outweigh the benefits and impart an overall disadvantage. Choice *A* would affect all spiders, not just the painted spider. Choice *B* strengthens the argument rather than weakens it. Choice *C* does not affect the argument either way, and there is no information about the effect of web size on catching ability (and it sounds like there's uniformity in the size of painted spiders' webs and other spiders' webs anyway), so Choice *E* can be eliminated as well.

2. B: Choice *B* includes the reason the argument is flawed: just because evidence in support of the hypothesis (that there is extraterrestrial life in the universe) has not yet been found, does not conclusively indicate that the hypothesis is necessarily wrong. Due to the immense vastness and other technological, financial, and practical limitations, it's quite difficult to explore space. It is perfectly reasonable that evidence simply has yet to be found.

3. B: Bart's conclusion is that the supercomputer's result is unacceptable because the process by which it was obtained cannot be understood. Therefore, the assumption is laid out in Choice *B:* for a mathematical result to be acceptable, the process by which it was obtained must be understandable to someone. Choice *A* is incorrect because Bart does not seem to find solutions derived by supercomputers to be inherently unacceptable. Choice *C* deals more with Anne's concerns, not Bart's. Choice *D* makes a new assumption that acceptability would be guaranteed. Choice *E* assumes the supercomputer cannot find a solution via an understandable process, but we do not have the information to be sure of that.

4. C: Bart and Anne are at odds about what constitutes the criterion to be used for accepting mathematical results derived by supercomputers. Bart argues that they must be understandable by humans to be valid, and Anne argues they simply need to be reproducible by other supercomputers.

5. D: Choice *A* is not supported by the example in the passage with the food oil competitors because sales dropped for all food oils. Be careful of extreme language like "in all cases." There is nothing in the passage that is related to Choices *B* or *E*. Like Choice *A,* Choice *C* has extreme language— "under no circumstances"—this conclusion is an unreasonable jump.

6. C: Choice *C* raises a reason why the increased water in reservoirs will still be inefficient for the demand. In fact, it raises two reasons: increased population (increased demand) and an inability to pump the water fast enough to meet that demand. Accordingly, rationing will still be necessary to help stay within the pumping means and ability to supply water. Choice *A* does not undermine the prediction. Choice *B* is irrelevant. Choice *D* would potentially lead to changes in water usage, but there is not enough information to anticipate the effects. Choice *E* would affect all summers—and theoretically, they haven't all required rationing—so it isn't as strong of a response.

7. A: Judy's response does not restate the evidence John did, so Choice *B* is incorrect. Choice *C* is incorrect because although it gives additional evidence, what Judy says does not support John's conclusion. Choice *D* is incorrect because John's assumption is not that whenever people drive more than five miles from home, they are going on a long trip. Choice *E* is not reflective of Judy's response.

8. B: If only unreasonable people adapt the world to them and this is the hypothetical criterion for progress, if there are only reasonable people, it holds that progress will not occur. This is described in Choice *B.* The statements don't support the conclusion in Choice *A.* Choice *C* makes an unjustified assumption. The passage doesn't say that only *some* unreasonable people can bring about progress, so Choice *D* is not supported by the statements. Choice *E* is not found in the statements.

9. A: Choice *A* is the only answer choice that addresses the producer's behavior in focusing on the effect of the critique rather than its content. With this, the producer is then speculating an outcome rather than addressing the critic's poor experience and trying to reshape their view. Additionally, the producer is employing a sort of blaming logic in trying to convince the critic to refrain from positing their review. Compared to all of the other answer choices (which address tangible concerns within the scenario) Choice *A* is the more questionable.

10. A: It makes sense that if da Volterra removed all of the layers of paint (including Michelangelo's) already before he added his personal additions to the Sistine Chapel, the restorers would not be interested in reviving de Volterra's additions, as there'd be nothing left under them from Michelangelo or otherwise. Thus, Choice *A* is correct. Choices *B* and *C* point to reasons why da Volterra's work might be workable in the Sistine Chapel, but they ignore the ultimate goal, which is to uncover Michelangelo's original work. The rationale given in Choice *A* is superior because it addresses this priority. Choices *D* and *E*, again, focuses on a potential positive of de Volterra's work, but it still misses the ultimate goal of uncovering Michelangelo's work.

11. E: It is unclear if the inmates know their behavior can afford them this benefit, motivating some to act better than they would otherwise, or if well-behaving inmates are offered the benefit at some point unbeknownst to them. Either way, there is reason to believe this sample is not representative because the conclusion drawn relies on the assumption that all inmates were just as likely to be initially selected in the sample that got the surgery. In reality, it seems more probable that inmates already more motivated to change their lives or behave better were in the surgery sample group. Thus, it's not necessarily the surgery itself—but the person getting the procedure's motivation and conscience—that has influenced their post-release crime rate.

12. A: Choice *A* raises an overlooked aspect that would confound the reasoning in the argument. If there are eye diseases that can alter the pattern of blood vessels in the retina, the unique, fingerprint-like nature of this pattern would no longer be detectable by the scanner as that same, previously-scanned individual.

13. B: Choice *B* helps justify the conclusion that Earth's moon was not formed from an inner piece of the Earth and the statements in the passage indicated it also does not have many similar crust materials. Choice *A* does not affect the conclusion drawn either way because the statements in the passage do not say the moons of all planets in a solar system must be formed the same way. Choice *C* does not help justify the conclusion that Earth's moon was not formed from an inner piece of the Earth. Choice *D* points to the idea that maybe the Earth/moon system is in an area hit by meteoroids, but the last sentence of the stimulus still raises the issues with the idea that Earth's moon does not seem to be formed by the same materials as Earth. Choice *E* is irrelevant.

14. E: In order for this to be evidence for the hypothesis presented, the caffeine-producing plants, at some point, must have been preyed upon by insects, building a need to develop a protection. This adaptation would not have been perpetuated as an evolutionary advantage if it was not a problem in the first place. The other answer choices are not assumptions that the argument necessarily relies upon.

15. C: The pattern of reasoning in the stimulus is that only a specific one type of plant (tulip) was in the garden, and only a subtype (tall ones) at that, so the *only* plants in the garden are tall tulips. This is mirrored in Choice *C*. Only one type of primate is at the zoo (gorilla) and *only* a subtype of that group (small ones), so the only primates at the zoo are small gorillas. Choice *A* uses very similar wording and reasoning, but the last clause uses the verbiage "all of the dogs in the show were black" instead of "the *only* dogs in the show were black." Choice *B* uses different reasoning. Choice *D*, like Choice *A*, uses very similar wording and reasoning to the stimulus statements, but the last clause uses the verbiage "none of" instead of "the *only* fruit in the kitchen was not ripe." Choice *E* follows a different pattern of reasoning.

16. C: To be able to properly infer something from a statement, you must be able to point to evidence to back that up. Choice *C* is the only answer where this is possible. The whole basis of the original statement is that funding cannot be properly provided based on scientific merit and on political considerations at the same time. This means they must be incompatible with one another.

17. A: Choice *A* provides a reason why the new vacuums enabled with the active silencer would be lower electricity consumption possible. With the new, superior silencers, which can actively reduce the sound waves emitted from the device, these louder, yet more energy-efficient motors can replace the quieter, more energy-demanding ones; thus, lowering the energy consumption of the appliance. Choice *B* would actually increase the energy consumed and emitted by the appliance. The other choices provide reasons that are not supportive as to why the new device would lower electricity consumption. Choice *E* would theoretically add the same device-induced weight to the appliance.

18. D: Choice *D* weakens the argument because it's possible the dinosaurs in Arctic (and all) regions were still cold-blooded reptiles but that the need to prevent starvation and thus migrate to undesirable places and climates, superseded the energy-inefficiency or even die-off of some group members from being too cold to survive. Choice *A* mostly strengthens the argument, providing evidence that current cold-blooded reptiles apparently have to live in warm climates to withstand thermoregulation. Choice *B* does not impact the argument. Choices *C* and *E* strengthen the argument by providing evidence that the Arctic was indeed as cold (or colder) than as it is today, meaning the risk of cold-blooded dinosaurs freezing to death was a real possibility.

19. A: Maria's main concern is that the denotation of the term "totalitarian" does not match the political system to which it is being assigned in practice with exact precision. This mismatch in what is expected, based on the strict definition, and its use to categorize real-life scenarios can cause mislead expectations. Arguably, Choices *B, C, D,* and *E* are expressed in her comments, but they are not her main concern. It is the discrepancy between what is described by the official definition and the looseness of the term's practical application that most concern's Maria.

20. D: James disputes—and then suggests alternative—conditions under which "totalitarian" can be appropriately applied. James broadens the applicability of the term in real-life practice and removes some of the extreme denotative strictness and precision of Maria's viewpoint. The other answer choices do not accurately describe James' response.

21. D: Choice *A* is too extreme; the passage does not indicate that body features must be *identical* in one class of organisms in a certain environment. There is also nothing to support the conclusion in Choice *B*. Choice *C* uses extreme language that we can't fully substantiate as a claim from the statements in the stimulus. It might be that there are other stimuli that lead to convergence in terms of external body structures between different classes of organisms; environmental conditions might not be the *only* known cause, and the passage does not address this. Choice *E* makes too much of a blanket statement than can be properly inferred; here, again, we do not have enough evidence from the passage to support this choice.

22. B: Here we are looking for a pattern of reasoning that matches the statement. The pattern of reasoning in the original statement was that an event occurred that wasn't previously known about and as a result a new conclusion could be formed. Choice *B* is also presented in the same manner. Since Turner is now in Nantes at 11, it can be concluded that she had to take a different train to do so.

23. D: Of the ethical criteria described in the answer choices, Choice *D* would best support the journalist's conclusion while allowing the report to flow. In this case, because the cause of the starvation wasn't a "known fact," in that there was a lack of clear evidence as to a natural cause or errant governmental withholding, it is *not* unethical (meaning it is ethical) to withhold the information as long as a censorship alert precedes the report. The journalist was planning to include a notice of censorship, so he or she is acting in line with this answer choice.

24. B: Maternal age greater than 40 is a minority subset of all babies born. The argument overlooks this fact. Choice *A* is incorrect because the argument does not appear to assume what it sets out to establish. Choices *C* and *D* do not ultimately affect the argument either way, and do not affect the conclusion. Choice *E* would be interesting to learn, but does not really capture the problem with the argument.

25. C: The argument infers that since the two institutions are similar in that they both involve working for another's purpose rather than the worker's own, they are both similar in another respect or factor (in this case, the degree to which they are pernicious, which means harmful or damaging, especially gradually over the long term). The other choices are not argumentative techniques used in this particular argument.

26: A: With voluntary labor, the laborer is still achieving some benefits that theoretically should align with his or her personal purpose, making a majority of the money per hour for himself or herself, not the government. However, in forced servitude, the servant is working primarily for his or her "master" and has little personal say over their decisions. Theoretically, regular labor is volitional; the worker has selected the job because it presumably satisfies their own "purpose." Choice *B* is incorrect because the author would still argue the same point regardless of the specific tax rate because in the author's opinion, any money paid in the way of taxes to the government is for another's purpose. Choice *C* is wrong because the author does not specifically state that all work is taxed; the author is just talking about the labor that is. Choice *D* is a separate argument but not one necessarily applicable here as an "error in reasoning." Choice *E* is incorrect because the author is not ultimately altering definitions with subjective opinions.

Section 4

1. B: The author focuses on the personal and emotional nature of Byron's poetry and how his poetry speaks of him. The author says things like "different characters speak in his poems, but finally it is usually he himself who is speaking" and that he has "a close presence in his poetry." This is well-reflected in Choice *B*. Choice *A* is incorrect because although the author discusses Byron's "lax literary method" and Byron not being a "great" poet, this is not the main idea of the passage. Choices *C, D,* and *E* are much broader than the scope and focus of this passage.

2. D: Just as the author mentions Escarpit's 1958 work as an example of one type of writing on Byron, so too does the other mention Russell and Praz to provide examples of writers on another category of writing about Byron. Choices *A, B,* and *C* do not appear in conjunction with mentioning Russell and Praz in the passage. Choice *E* is the most appealing alternative, but the author doesn't qualify the merit of Russell and Praz's work, such that we cannot conclude that the author necessarily feels these are the "best studies" of Byron's work.

3. C: Clearly, the author is invested in considering Byron's personal, emotional connection to his own poetry. As stated in the first paragraph, the author believes Byron's poems "record the emotional pressure of certain moments in his life." Therefore, it's reasonable to assume that the author would be keen to see a study aiming to identify the emotions Byron felt at certain times in his life. He could then look at how the poetry he created during these periods reflected those emotions.

4. C: The first paragraph introduces the idea that there are three types of studies that have been conducted on Byron—biographical, ideas-related, and poetry-centric. The remainder of the paragraph focuses in on the last of these and discusses the shortcomings of many studies of Byron's poetry and how literary studies should of his work should differ from other poets who write with less of an emotional slant.

5. C: Whenever trying to effectively make a claim or build an argument, authors must supply supporting details to substantiate their ideas. The author of this passage is asserting that "Byron's literary craftsmanship is irregular" as another piece of supportive evidence (in addition to the statement that the majority of Byron's "cannot be convincingly read as subtle verbal creations") that he is not a "great" poet. Choice *A* might be seen as appealing because the author does contrast the poetic works of Byron and Shakespeare in the prior paragraph, but he or she does not explicitly state that Shakespeare *is* one of "great" poets nor is the author only comparing Byron's poetic skill and irregular literary craftsmanship with Shakespeare directly and not "great" poets in general. Choice *D* is not a function of that quote. While Choice *E* uses language seen in the sentence preceding the one in question, this quote does not serve as an explanation of that preceding point, just a second point.

6. E: The author suggests that most of Shakespeare's poems can be read without instigating the reader's curiosity about the factors in the author's personal life that motivated the poet to author their work as evidenced by his statement at the end of the first paragraph. Choice *A* may seem correct, but the author does speak nothing directly of this in the passage and the question stem hinges on the author's opinion. Choices *B* and *D* are essentially contradictions of the author's words. Choice *C* takes thing too far. We aren't told definitively that Shakespeare's works unilaterally do not reflect, and are not connected to, the poet's real-life events and emotions. Instead, the author suggests there to be a general trend of impersonality and a lack of motivation from life events behind Shakespeare's work.

7. B: In line 5, after citing the example of Escarpit's 1958 biographical study of Byron's psychology and life events, directly states that "biographers to this day continue to speculate about Byron's life." Therefore, Choice *B* is correct.

8. A: Readers will note that beginning on line 33, the author answers the question as to what he or she considers to be the primary enjoyment in reading Byron's poetry when he or she says, "If Byron is not a "great" poet, his poetry is nonetheless of extradentary interest to us because of the pleasure it gives us." The author goes on to explain why Byron's poetry brings this pleasure and that pleasure in reading the work of a poet is valuable. Choice *B* is wrong; while the author mentions others who have studied Byron, these individuals are measured more in passing and as examples. The author does not provide information regarding whether these such individuals dedicated most of their professional study on Byron. Choice *C* is likely a question the author *wants* to answer, but the passage does not yet specifically answer that. Choices *D* and *E* are not answered in the passage.

9. E: Directly after the passage states that the United States Supreme Court "has not always resolved legal issues of concern to Native Americans in a manner that has pleased the Indian nations" it answers the very question posed here by giving the reason that "many of the Court's decisions have been products of political compromise."

10. A: The author states in lines 12-14 that the "power of the Supreme Court has been exercised in a manner that has been usually beneficial to Native Americans." The critics mentioned in line 18 hold an opposing viewpoint to this generally favorable one and are thus, leery of the United States Supreme Court's treatment of Native American affairs. They believe the Supreme Court has used a "patronizing tone" and demonstrate an "apparent rejection of Native American values as important points to consider when reviewing a case." Accordingly, the objections from such critics would best be satisfied by a Supreme Court decision that demonstrated respect for Native Americans as people and for the principles and qualities they deem important.

11. C: While the author might agree with some of the sentiments in the other choices, such as Choices *A, B,* and *E,* the author does not specifically call the judicial system of the United States "accommodating". Instead, the author is providing the particular situation of political compromise as a reason why the judicial system has an "accommodating" nature.

12. B: The author describes a generally favorable or appreciative attitude toward the United States Supreme Court's decisions regarding legal issues of concerns to Native Americans; of the answer choices, this tone is best reflected in Choice *B,* restrained appreciation. The author states that the Court's decisions have "usually been beneficial" to Native Americans and "favor the rights" of Native American litigants. Choice *A,* wholehearted endorsement, is too enthusiastic or positive of a descriptor of the author's attitude. Choice *C* is also incorrect. "Detached objectivity" reflects an impartial, dispassionate, and unemotional attitude. This passage is steeped with emotion and opinion. Choices *D* and *E* are on the opposite end of the attitude spectrum from where the author's impression of the situation seems to lie. Thus, they are both incorrect.

13. D: Choices *A, B,* and *E* are incorrect they are either not mentioned in the paragraph or directly opposed by what is written. Choice *C* is also incorrect because the paragraph explains how the federal government believes states' powers should be minimal; thus, it can be inferred that author would not believe it is in the best interest of Native Americans to have their affairs decided more strongly by the state.

14. E: The author's primary purpose in this passage is to raise and support a contention with evidence and rationale. The passage mentions some opposing views and opinions, but this is not the focus, so Choices *A* and *C* are incorrect. Similarly, it does not spend much time or attention assessing claims made by disputants. Thus, Choice *D* is incorrect. There is little to no reevaluation of traditional beliefs, so Choice *B* is incorrect.

15. B: As stated in lines 12-14, the author believes the "power of the Supreme Court has been exercised in a manner that has been usually beneficial to Native Americans." Then, he or she goes on to provide examples of the exercise of judicial power used for the benefit or equitable treatment of Native Americans, as a way to provide evidence against critics of this opinion. Therefore, it can be inferred that the author believes that the Supreme Court's treatment of Native American affairs has been reasonably supportive in most situations.

16. C: Test takers should always be wary of extreme language like "always," "never," "any," "all," or "none," in answer choices. For example, even the sentence in lines 28-29 says that "By studying a specific area of the pile, one can even **predict** whether avalanches will occur there in the near future." Therefore, it is incorrect to conclude that the author believes it would be impossible to make any prediction about large interactive systems. Although, of course, the systems are not sandpile avalanches, the author has painted this analogy and used it to explain the challenge of predicting catastrophes.

17. E: The author contests that criticality is a "global property of the sandpile." Critical readers can identify supporting details that provide evidence for this claim, such as in the description of adding sand grains to the pile versus the ones lost (lines 37-45). As stated, "the system reaches its critical state when the amount of sand added is balanced, on average, by the amount falling off the edge..."

18. A: The theory referenced is that the investigators believed that the response a disturbance in large interactive systems is proportional to the disturbance (because it tends to be for small systems). Therefore, because a grain of sand is so miniscule, such a theory would predict that it would not cause anything beyond a minor disturbance. The other answer choices are not supported by the theory stated in the second paragraph nor the sand analogy explanation that follows in the subsequent paragraphs.

19. E: Choice *E* best describes the general organization of the passage. The passage opens by describing a traditional method of analyzing catastrophes in large interactive systems and the reasons for employing this method (mainly due to its success in small systems). The passage then introduces an alternative method or way to consider the situation via an example (the sandpile). None of the other choices accurately reflect the passage's organization.

20. E: The investigators "believed they could predict the behavior of large interactive systems by studying its elements separately and by analyzing its component mechanisms individually." This most closely mirrors the engineer who analyzes each structural element of a bridge to draw conclusions about the structural soundness of the bridge overall.

21. D: The bulk of the passage is dedicated to explaining and expounding upon the new theoretical approach to the previously poor model. We can infer that the author is most concerned with describing this new approach based on the time, attention, and detail proportionally dedicated to this aspect of the passage.

22. C: *A* is incorrect because the third paragraph discusses ways in which the new scholarship has poked holes in the former theory and has focused more on a comprehensive view of colonial women, rather than just considered their economic status, as was previously the case. The error in Choice *B* is that the recent studies have not altered the "golden age" theory, but rather formed new, separate theories and ways of considering the status of colonial women. In Choice *D,* while the answer choice is somewhat true, it is not the *best* summary of passage's main point. Choice *E* is incorrect because the author does not say that the issues with the earlier "golden age" theory were due to insufficient research.

23. D: The author mentions Joan Hoff-Wilson as an example of a historian who seemingly rejected the "golden age" theory, yet still perpetuated and ascribed to the belief that nineteenth century middle-class women did experience a "loss of function and authentic status." This is to say that the "golden age" theory persisted in the world of academia, even among historians who tended to consider themselves opposed to it or believers of a very evolved alternative (when, in fact, that alternative was quite similar).

24. C: The scholars mentioned in line 32 could be considered paradoxical because they purport rejecting the "golden age" theory, yet they continue to "accept the paradigm of a nineteenth-century decline from a more desirable past." Much like a paradox, this thinking is rather contradictory as the latter is merely a loose summary of the former. Thus, it doesn't make sense to reject one and ascribe to another when the two are essentially the same.

25. A: The "three-part chronological division" of colonial women's lives developed by more recent studies takes into account the breadth and multifactorial circumstances that should be considered when assessing the quality of colonial women's lives. The other answer choices are not supported by the passage.

26. A: The publications reveal that the Dexter's argument was too simplistic, "unsophisticated," and narrowly focused. These publications advocate for a much more well-rounded critique of colonial women's lives, extending far beyond the sole factor of economic status typified by Dexter's theory. The other answer choices reflect incorrect interpretations of the findings in these studies.

27. B: The "golden age" theory was closely dialed into the sole factor of economic status of colonial women wholly determining their social status. This is a far simpler, much less sophisticated rubric by which to assess their lives and standing in society than emerged from the studies of my recent scholars. As stated in line 48, "The new scholarship presents a farm more complicated picture, one in which definitions of gender roles, the colonial economy, demographic patterns, religion, the law, and household organization all contributed to defining the circumstances of colonial women's lives." Preceding this point is another salient one discussing the "golden age" theory being "simplistic and unsophisticated" basing its assessment of the status of colonial women "solely on one factor (their economic function in society) and assumed all too readily that a relatively simple social system automatically brought higher standing... ." Therefore, it's evident that practitioners of the new scholarship find fault with the simplistic nature of the former theory and its assumptions about status.

Greetings!

First, we would like to give a huge "thank you" for choosing us and this study guide for LSAT exam. We hope that it will lead you to success on this exam and for your years to come.

Our team has tried to make your preparations as thorough as possible by covering all of the topics you should be expected to know. We have also included many test-taking strategies to help you learn the material, maintain the knowledge, and take the test with confidence.

We strive for excellence in our products, and if you have any comments or concerns over the quality of something in this study guide, please send us an email so that we may improve.

As you continue forward in life, we would like to remain alongside you with other books and study guides in our library. We are continually producing and updating study guides in several different subjects. If you are looking for something in particular, all of our products are available on Amazon. You may also send us an email!

Sincerely,
APEX Test Prep
info@apexprep.com

FREE

Free Study Tips DVD

In addition to the tips and content in this guide, we have created a FREE DVD with helpful study tips to further assist your exam preparation. **This FREE Study Tips DVD provides you with top-notch tips to conquer your exam and reach your goals.**

Our simple request in exchange for the strategy-packed DVD is that you email us your feedback about our study guide. We would love to hear what you thought about the guide, and we welcome any and all feedback—positive, negative, or neutral. It is our #1 goal to provide you with top-quality products and customer service.

To receive your **FREE Study Tips DVD**, email freedvd@apexprep.com. Please put "FREE DVD" in the subject line and put the following in the email:

> a. The name of the study guide you purchased.
>
> b. Your rating of the study guide on a scale of 1-5, with 5 being the highest score.
>
> c. Any thoughts or feedback about your study guide.
>
> d. Your first and last name and your mailing address, so we know where to send your free DVD!

Thank you!

Printed in the USA
CPSIA information can be obtained
at www.ICGtesting.com
LVHW080008110923
757664LV00016B/1588